"For weeks after that fight I was a victim to nightmare. In the middle of my sleep I would jump up in bed, my eyeballs starting from my head, my hair on end, my face and body dripping with perspiration. Imagining myself surrounded by shrieking, savage Zulus on the point of plunging their cruel assegais into me."

Henry Hook VC, *The Sketch*, 20 April 1898.

ACKNOWLEDGMENTS

Thank you to Sheldon Hall for allowing me to quote from his book, *Zulu: With Some Guts Behind It*, including permission to reproduce his speech, made during the rededication of Hook's grave. Acknowledgement is also given to Barry Johnson whose exceptional research on Hook was a source of inspiration, and to Paul Barnett and Wilf Charles for supplying information and photographs. As always, Ron Sheeley supplied some excellent images from his extensive collection.

Henry Hook VC
A Rorke's Drift Hero

Neil Thornton

BARNTHORN
PUBLISHING

CONTENTS

INTRODUCTION

Upon its release on 22 January 1964, the movie, *Zulu,* brought the Anglo-Zulu War to the attention of the public with a stirring action-packed depiction of the Battle of Rorke's Drift. Released on the 85th anniversary of the battle, it boasted a star-studded cast and a magnificent score. The film has stood the test of time and now holds 'classic' status. Yet, as with most war movies based on real events, discrepancies and inaccuracies are commonplace. In the case of *Zulu,* almost all the characters differ from their real-life counterparts, particularly Private Henry Hook, who featured onscreen as a man who shirked his duty and was considered a troublemaker by his officers and NCOs.[1]

Hook was portrayed as a hard-drinking rogue. One particular scene showed him breaking into a cabinet mid-battle for a bottle of liquor. Yet, the real Hook was known for his excellent conduct and whilst in South Africa he had taken a pledge not to drink alcohol.

Hook never forgot Rorke's Drift and it remained at the forefront of his mind until the day he died. Indeed, when he passed away shortly after moving back to Gloucestershire from London, a large engraving of de Neuville's painting, 'The Defence of Rorke's Drift', was hanging above his bed in his new home. Neither did he forget those comrades who had fought alongside him, and in later years, even when suffering from ill-health, he would make every effort to attend reunions and special commemorative occasions.

The Battle of Rorke's Drift was the stand-out event in Hook's life and the outstanding courage and steadfastness that he displayed on that occasion, have immortalised Henry Hook's name through the annuls of history.

This is his story.

1

BACKGROUND

Born in Churcham, Huntley, near Gloucester on 6 August 1850, Alfred Henry Hook–known by his middle name of Henry throughout his life–was one of six children to Henry and Ellen Hook (nee Higgs).[2] His father was an agricultural labourer and they lived at a place called 'Birdwood' which was popularly known as 'Hooks' Farm'.

By the age of ten, young Henry was, according to the census, a woodcutter, as was his father. Henry enlisted into the Royal Monmouth Militia on 7 May 1869 and would serve with them for five years. On Boxing Day 1870, he married Comfort Jones and they soon began a family. Raymond John was born in October 1871, followed by Mary Henrietta in September 1873, and finally Julia Ann, born in May 1876.

Records state that Hook joined the 25th Brigade at Monmouth on 13 March 1877 and attested at Brecon on the same day as a private soldier in 'B' Company, 2nd Battalion, 24th (2nd Warwickshire) Regiment (referred to hereafter as 2/24th, where the 1st Battalion will appear as 1/24th). Like most of 'B' Company who would come to fight at Rorke's Drift, and indeed like many soldiers throughout the army, Hook gave his occupation as 'labourer' when attesting.

In June 1964, after the release of *Zulu*, *The Beacon* newspaper in Brecon reported that Hook had found himself in front of the magistrates and, having been given the option of going to jail or enlisting in the army, he had chosen the latter.[3]

The same rumour persists with Fred Hitch, another VC recipient who fought alongside Hook at Rorke's Drift. Hitch attested in London at the Marlborough Police Court, and the story has evidently stemmed from this. However, it was not uncommon for men to enlist at administrative centres such as these. Many soldiers did so, including a number of 'Rorke's Drift men' who served with the battalion. In 1871, like Fred Hitch, James Keefe also attested at Marlborough Police Court. He was just fourteen years of age at the time and was posted as a 'boy' to the 2/24th.

Other men who attested at police courts who would go on to fight at Rorke's Drift include William Davis and Edward Robinson, both of whom attested at Bow Street Police Court in London. Incidentally, both did have rather poor conduct records during their military careers. Two other Rorke's Drift men–George Shearman and seventeen-year-old William Dicks both attested at Westminster Police Court. The conduct of these two men would also be questionable and they would invariably find themselves in trouble throughout their service. Yet in all cases, there is no evidence to confirm that any of them were given the option of choosing military service over detainment.

Posted to the 2/24th, Hook had been a member of the battalion for less than a year when, in February 1878, he found himself sailing for the Cape as a member of 'B' Company for active service.

The Ninth Cape Frontier War (or Xhosa War) was one of a series of small wars between Britain's empire and the Xhosa Kingdom that spanned 100 years up until 1878. With no open battles and faced with an enemy that preferred skirmishes rather than fighting outright, the war was in stark contrast to what they would experience in the coming war with the Zulus. Hook never went into detail about his personal experiences during this war, but much bush fighting took place in which 'B' Company was heavily involved.

On 9 May, whilst climbing some rocks, their company commander, Captain Godwin-Austen, was wounded when the rifle of one of his NCOs 'exploded' behind him.[4] The bullet caught Godwin-Austen in the back, and he was carted away, destined to miss not only the remainder of the Cape War but also the Zulu War where his company, under the command of Lieutenant Gonville Bromhead who took over in his absence, would enter the annuls of military history for their fight with the with the Zulus at Rorke's Drift.

On 21 July 1878, the battalion received orders to embark immediately for Natal. With a war with the Zulus looking imminent, they moved within days and after disembarking at Durban, marched on to Pietermaritzburg where they arrived on 6 August.

By now Hook was fully accustomed to the climate and the hardships and sickness that came with it. But he and his comrades were not prepared for the enemy they were about to face.

2

RORKE'S DRIFT

Hook, like all the men of 'B' Company, 2/24th, was disappointed at finding himself stuck at Rorke's Drift. The central column of the invasion force, made up of the 1st and 2nd Battalions of the 24th Foot, as well as various other units, had crossed the Buffalo River at Rorke's Drift on 11 January to seek out and defeat King Cetshwayo's Zulu Army (impi). The column, numbering just shy of 5,000 men from a variety of units, was under the command of Colonel Glyn, 1/24th, but his leadership was somewhat undermined by the presence of Commander-In-Chief, Lord Chelmsford who, accompanied them with his staff.

Like 'G' Company, 2/24th, that found itself undertaking garrison duty at Helpmekaar 10 miles further back in Natal, 'B' Company had drawn the short straw and for the time being were under orders to guard the Rorke's Drift mission station which was in use as a supply depot and staging post for the invasion.

The Rorke's Drift mission station owed its name to the original owner, James Rorke, who had purchased the land in the 1840's and built his home with accompanying storehouse from which he used to trade. Since then, ownership had changed hands several times. By 1879, the station was under the ownership of The Church of Sweden who leased it to the British for their invasion. Reverend Otto Witt lived there with his family who resided in the house, whilst the old storehouse had been converted into a chapel. A hill overlooking the mission station, known as Shiyane had been renamed as the Oscarsberg by Witt in honour of the Swedish King. With the hustle and bustle of the military presence, Witt's family had moved away for the time being, whilst Witt himself remained behind.

The British invasion force utilised the chapel as a storehouse which had been its original purpose, and Witt's house was used as a hospital under the charge of Surgeon James Reynolds, an experienced army surgeon who had served alongside the 24th Regiment during the Ninth Cape Frontier War.

Shortly after the column had crossed the border, a few casualties arrived at the Rorke's Drift hospital following a skirmish at the homestead of a Zulu chief, Sihayo kaXongo, but most of the thirty-six patients were suffering from sicknesses and a variety of ailments connected to the climate and conditions. Dysentery and fever were rife.

Since the column had moved on, things were generally quiet at Rorke's Drift, at least for the soldiers of the 24th. Wagons and men came and went as supplies were moved forward to join the column, but none of this concerned Bromhead's men who made themselves busy by playing cards, writing letters home, and anything else they could think of to pass the time.

On the morning of 19 January, Lieutenant John Chard, 5th (Field) Company, Royal Engineers, arrived with his driver (his batman, Charles Robson), a corporal, and three sappers after being ordered to move forward ahead of his company with instructions to join the column as soon as possible. Chard pitched his tents by the ponts–'floating bridges' as Hook called them–at the river-crossing, situated about half a mile away, out of sight of the mission station.

Lieutenant John Chard, R.E., who would hold overall command at Rorke's Drift during the battle.

3

ISANDLWANA

Unlike the men left at Rorke's Drift, the mood of the advancing column was altogether cheerier. The men knew they were soon to do battle with the Zulus. Of course, the worry that the Zulus would not be willing to meet in open battle was unfounded. On the morning of 22 January, after being discovered in a deep ravine several miles from the camp, King Cetshwayo's Impi rose from the ground and charged the unsuspecting British camp. Unbeknown to the Zulus at the time, Lord Chelmsford, during the hours of darkness, had led roughly half the column from the camp in pursuit of what he believed to be the Zulu Impi. Those left in the camp were overwhelmed, with virtually all the redcoats being killed.

***

That morning, Lieutenant Chard had been unsure of his orders. His sappers had been kept busy trying to get a second pont operational but late the previous evening he had received an order from the column to say the men of the Royal Engineers were to proceed to iSandlwana at once. The order was ambiguous and did not specify whether Chard himself should accompany them. To clarify the matter, he rode out ahead of his engineers who were moving slowly in their wagon, to see if his presence was required.

Upon arriving, Chard discovered that he was not needed at the camp and was to return to the river at Rorke's Drift where a company of 1/24th under Captain Rainforth was due to arrive and entrench itself overlooking the crossing point. He was handed a copy of his orders detailing specific tasks he was to carry out. Before he began his return journey, Chard spoke to an NCO of the 24th. Looking through their field glasses the two men observed what Chard described as 'the enemy moving on the distant hills, and apparently in great force.'[5]

To bolster the strength of the camp at iSandlwana, Colonel Durnford who had been camped just over the Zulu side of the river with his unit of Natal Native Contingent (NNC), was ordered to move forward. Chard, when on his way back to Rorke's Drift from iSandlwana, passed him on the road and a little later, after meeting with his own engineers, had them walk with Durnford's men whilst he took the wagon back to the ponts.

Upon his return Chard rode up to the mission station and reported what he had seen to Major Spalding who held command of Rorke's Drift and the line of communication to Helpmekaar. Captain Rainforth was overdue and with Zulus being sighted Spalding was concerned that they still hadn't arrived. Therefore, he decided to ride back to hurry them along, hoping to have them in place before dark should the Zulus try to move on the ponts. Before departing, Spalding checked the army list and found that Chard had been commissioned in 1868 and Bromhead in 1871, therefore, Chard–having held his commission for the longest–would be in charge whilst Spalding was away.

At Rorke's Drift, Hook was kept busy brewing tea for the patients in the hospital. Amongst them was Sergeant Robert Maxfield, 2/24th, a Monmouth man, whose mother ran a small shop in the town centre right by the Hook family home. Maxfield was suffering terribly from fever to such an extent that he was completely unaware of his surroundings and very confused.

The patients' beds were nothing more than thin wooden boards with straw placed on top. They lay on the floor about six inches from the ground.

The role of hospital cook had probably fallen to Hook through a rotation system. Fred Hitch whose name falls next to Hook's on the company roster was carrying out the same job for the active men of the company, suggesting it was simply their turn and the tasks went to whomever was next alphabetically on the roster list.

The sounds of gunfire from the direction of iSandlwana in the afternoon caused little concern to the men at Rorke's Drift. Bromhead was sat with Assistant-Commissary Walter Dunne, of the Commissariat and Transport Department, enjoying lunch under an awning that they had propped up to protect themselves from the sun. Down at the ponts, Chard was also unperturbed by recent events. He had settled nicely by the river and was writing a letter home whilst enjoying a relaxing lunch.

Meanwhile, Surgeon Reynolds together with Otto Witt and a Chaplain to the Forces, Reverend George Smith, had scaled the Oscarsberg to try to see what was happening at iSandlwana.

Hook, meanwhile, was still preparing tea for the patients when he received a nasty and unexpected shock:

> Between three and four in the afternoon, when I was engaged preparing the tea for the sick at the out-of-door cooking place, just at the back of the hospital—for I was hospital cook—two mounted men, looking much exhausted, and their horses worn out, rode up to me. One was in his shirt sleeves, and without a hat, with a revolver strapped round his breast; the other had his coat and hat on. They stopped for a moment and told me that the whole force on the other side of the river had been cut up, and that the Zulus were coming on in great force.[6]

Hook was over at the south-side of the station behind the hospital and one of the first to hear the news from the fugitives. Hurrying into the camp Hook reported what he had heard. Others rushed in to do the same, and the place was soon alive with excitement. Fugitives continued to arrive with their own words of warning.

Bromhead and Dunne had been puzzled by the appearance of a large body of mounted natives some distance across the river, with some women, children, and oxen in front of them. Before they could investigate, the two men had been called back by a soldier who said a mounted infantryman wanted to see the officer in command. Upon Bromhead identifying himself, the man informed him that the iSandlwana camp had been taken by the Zulus.

Bromhead held an urgent discussion with Dunne and James Langley Dalton—a vastly experienced former-soldier now working under Walter Dunne in the Commissariat and Transport Department. Surgeon Reynolds was with them too, having rushed down from the Oscarsberg after seeing the riders coming in and wondering if they needed urgent medical attention, whilst Otto Witt and Reverend Smith had remained on the hill, oblivious to what was now happening around them.

One fugitive brought a note, written by an officer—Captain Gardner of the 14th Hussars who had escaped the field—telling them to 'fortify and hold the house.'[7] It was quickly decided that the post should be barricaded and defended against the imminent Zulu attack. The decision was made by Bromhead after various options had been discussed, although it was Dalton who had asserted this was the best course of action.

There is often confusion as to how things played out once the news of the disaster reached Rorke's Drift. At least one author has claimed that Chard and Bromhead had wanted to flee to Helpmekaar and were going to do so until Dalton stepped in to advise them to stay. As will be seen later, contradictions in Hook's various accounts have inadvertently been a major factor in this confusion.

In fact, after word of iSandlwana reached the post, the decision to stay was made at a time when Chard was still down by the river. This is confirmed in various sources, including Chard himself and Surgeon Reynolds who said:

> Lieutenant Bromhead, Acting Commissary Dalton, and myself forthwith consulted together, Lieutenant Chard not having as yet joined us from the pontoon, and we quickly decided that with barricades well placed around our present position a stand could be made where we were.'[8]

Reynolds went on to say that 'removing the sick and wounded would have been embarrassing to our movement, and desertion of them was never thought of.'[9]

Once the decision to stay and fight had been made and preparations for the defence had started, 'Lieutenant Chard arrived as this work was in progress and gave many useful orders as regards the lines of defence.'[10]

As alluded to by Reynolds, discussion must have taken place regarding the possibility of moving the hospital patients to Helpmekaar. Hook, in one of his later accounts, went one further by saying that before Chard had arrived, 'the camp was struck, and the two wagons loaded with sick men, ready to be driven off for greater safety to Helpmekaar.'[11] However, it was then decided that this was too hazardous 'as they would be almost certain to fall into the hands of the Zulus. The wagons therefore were unloaded, and helped to eke out the line of defence…'[12]

Reverend Smith concurred, stating in his own account written just days after the battle:

> A praiseworthy effort was made to remove the worst cases in hospital to a place of safety; two wagons were brought up, after some delay, and the patients were being brought out, when it was found that the Zulus were so close upon us that any attempt to take them away in ox-wagons would only result in their falling into the enemy's hands. So the two wagons were at once utilised and made to form part of the defensive wall...[13]

Hook, in an account given in 1898, related that a rider was sent to the river to inform Chard of the disaster and that 'pending his arrival, the camp was struck, and the two wagons loaded with sick men, ready to be driven off for greater safety to Helpmekaar.'[14]

He then went on to describe:

> On second thoughts it was judged too hazardous to attempt to move the sick to Helpmekaar, as they would be almost certain to fall into the hands of the Zulus.[15]

This account from Hook ties in with other accounts and would seem accurate.

However, in his last ever account, provided shortly before his death in 1905, Hook changed his story considerably:

> There was a general feeling that the only safe thing was to retire and try to join the troops at Helpmekaar. The horsemen had said that the Zulus would be up in two or three minutes; but luckily for us, they did not show themselves for more than an hour.
>
> Lieutenant Chard rushed up from the river, about a quarter of mile away, and saw Lieutenant Bromhead. Orders were given to strike the camp and make ready to go, and we actually loaded up two waggons. Then Mr. Dalton of the Commissariat Department, came up, and said that if we left the drift every man was certain to be killed. He had formerly been a sergeant-major in a Line regiment, and was one of the bravest men that ever lived.
>
> Lieutenants Chard and Bromhead held a consultation, short

and earnest; and orders were given that we were to get the hospital and storehouse ready for defence, and that we were never to say 'die' or 'surrender.'[16]

Those who claim that both Chard and Bromhead were on the verge of running away, use this one account as the basis to their argument, thus ignoring a multitude of primary sources–including Hook's own previous accounts–that state otherwise. As will be seen later, there are clear reasons for Hook's discrepancies.

Whilst it is true that Dalton played a major part in the barricading of the station, this was only done after all options had been discussed and ruled out, and on the orders of Bromhead who, in the absence of Chard, and as a regular infantry officer, held highest rank. It is distinctly possible, and indeed probable, that a general retirement to Helpmekaar was raised as an option, but so too was the possibility of meeting the Zulus in the open to fight it out, as suggested by Bromhead.[17]

Lieutenant Gonville Bromhead, 2/24th.

The 300 NNC at the station together with the men of the 24th quickly set to work building the perimeter with boxes of biscuits and mealie bags. The natives, however, were nervous and had to be persuaded at the point of the bayonet to carry out the work.

It was during this work that Lieutenant Chard arrived from the river, after receiving Bromhead's note and after hearing the new from two fugitives who had crossed at his ponts. Upon being informed of the plan to stay and fight, Chard agreed with the decision and quickly began adding his expertise to the developing perimeter.

Morale at the little garrison was lifted by the arrival of Captain Henderson with around 100 mounted infantry who Chard instructed to ride out to delay the Zulus for as long as possible, after which they were to return to help defend the mission station.

Whilst men rushed in and out of the storehouse with boxes and mealie bags to form the walls, Surgeon Reynolds hurriedly began preparing the hospital for defence. Although very much ill-suited for such a thing, there was no other option available as the storehouse was full of stock and a hive of activity as men rushed in and out carrying boxes and bags with which to build the barricades.

Yet, remarkably, despite admitting that the hospital was in a 'wretched position', Reynolds had complete faith that the building would hold, relating that there was a belief that, as long as the entire station wasn't overrun, the men in the building would hold out.[18]

Reynolds set to work preparing the hospital, noting that 'between the hospital orderlies, convalescent patients (8 or 10) and myself, we loop-holed the building and made a continuation of the commissariat defences round it.'[19] Lieutenant Bromhead oversaw the work to the barricades, but was also heavily involved preparing the buildings, Hook stating: 'Lieutenant Bromhead superintended the loopholing and barricading of the hospital and storehouse and the making of a connection of the defences between the two buildings with walls of mealie-bags and wagons.'[20]

At some point, Chard also entered the building and offered words of advice on how best to prepare. Grasping that the men in the rooms would be isolated, he asked them to 'mouse-hole'. In other words, he wanted them to knock through the internal walls to link the rooms which would allow movement from one to the other.

In his account to Queen Victoria, Chard wrote:

> I had tried to impress upon the men in the Hospital the necessity for making a communication right through the building—unfortunately this was not done. Probably at the time the men could not see the necessity, and doubtless also there was no time to do it.[21]

It seems that Hook and his five comrades hadn't yet been allocated the task of defending the hospital, although an account from Hook stating he himself made some loopholes could contradict this. Reynolds stated that he and the orderlies as well as the able-bodied patients were the ones who prepared it for defence, so Chard must have discussed it with some or all of these men. Whatever the case, the work was not carried out, and in a short space of time this decision not to 'mouse-hole' would result in loss of life for some of those in the hospital.

As preparations were underway, Otto Witt and Reverend Smith came rushing down from the hill. From their position on the summit, they had, for a time, been watching a large body of natives approach from the direction of iSandlwana. Unconcerned, they had thought the men were friendly natives, but as they drew nearer, realisation had dawned that the approaching force were Zulus. Finding the mission station in a state of urgency at the looming threat, Otto Witt entered his house (the hospital) to find his furniture being moved and the place barricaded. Mounting his horse, he quickly rode away to find his family. Reverend Smith would have joined him but after realising that his horse and his native groom had mysteriously vanished, he decided to remain to take part in the battle.

Henderson and his men came riding back to the station reporting that the Zulus were closing in and would be upon them shortly. The sight of the enemy proved too much for Henderson's men who, instead of stopping to assist in the defence, rode away, unwilling to face the Zulus twice in one day. Their actions greatly affected the nerve of the 300 natives working on the barricades who now decided to take off in the direction of Helpmekaar. Some men of the 24th opened fire on them as they ran, with one shot bringing down one of their NCOs, a corporal by the name of William Anderson.

Two defenders admitted that the men had fired shots at the fleeing natives which had struck a white NCO. One of these men was Fred Hitch. The other was Hook, who wrote: We were so enraged that we fired several shots at them, one of which dropped a European non-commissioned officer.[22] Reverend Smith also mentioned the episode, albeit in a more tactile yet less truthful manner by saying that Anderson was shot by Zulus who must have got into the garden.

Luckily, the defensive perimeter was virtually complete, but the loss of men convinced Chard that the perimeter was now too stretched. As a result, he ordered a second line of defence to be thrown up with biscuit boxes.

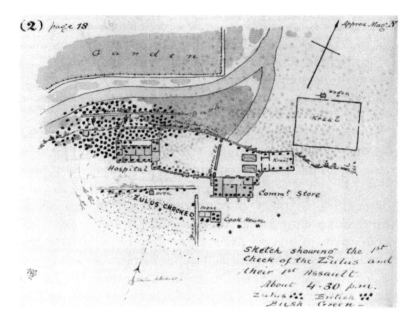

One of a series of diagrams sketched by Lieutenant Chard showing the defensive perimeter and the developments throughout the battle. The diagram shows an early stage in the engagement, after the section of wall in front of the hospital had been lost, but prior to the withdrawal from the main yard area. The Zulu attack came from the bottom (see directional arrow) before swinging to the left around the hospital to attack the front. Other points of interest in the sketch are the biscuit box wall dissecting the defence, the storehouse (bottom right of the perimeter), and also a cattle kraal to the right of the defence in which men were posted to defend. The larger kraal to the top right fell outside of the perimeter and was not defended.

When a couple of skirmish parties that had been sent out earlier came running back, it was clear to everyone that the time for battle was almost upon them.

Although most of the hospital patients were able to play an active role in the defence, shortly before the fighting started, six men of 'B' Company were ordered into the building to help defend it. It has been suggested in the past that these men may have volunteered for the task, but this was not the case. Each man was specifically ordered to do so.

In one account Hook related that he was 'placed in one of the corner rooms of the hospital.'[23] In another account he relates that, 'Half-a-dozen of us were stationed in the hospital, with orders to hold it and guard the sick', whilst William Jones, who was also tasked with defending the hospital, related that 'our officer, Lieutenant Bromhead, ordered six men into the hospital, myself being one of the number, to defend and rescue the sick from it.'[24,25] In another account, Jones stated that 'Lieutenant Bromhead, who was in charge of our small force, ordered six men to be sent to the hospital to defend it.'[26]

Bromhead may have been the one who issued the order, but it would seem that it was Colour-Sergeant Frank Bourne who relayed the order to the men. 'I was instructed to post men as look-outs, and in the hospital, and at the most vulnerable points…,' related Bourne.[27]

The six men selected to defend the hospital were split into three pairs and positioned at three corners of the building. The fourth corner was inside the perimeter and had no clear field of fire so did not need to be manned. The allotted hospital defenders were:

Pair No. 1 (south-east corner room)
William Jones. 2-24/593.
Robert Jones. 25B/716.

Pair No. 2 (south-west corner room)
Henry Hook. 25B/1373.
Thomas Cole. 25B/801.

Pair No.3 (north-west facing rooms)
John Williams (Fielding). 25B/1395
Joseph Williams. 25B/1398.

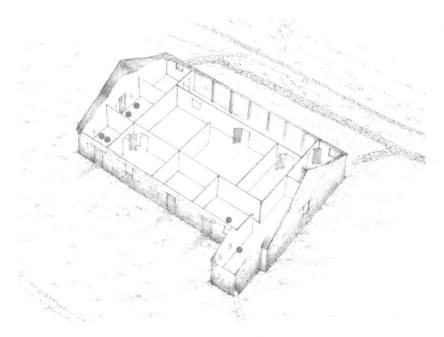

Diagram showing the starting positions of the six men allocated to defend the hospital. Hook and Cole were stationed in the corner room (far left), whilst John and Joseph Williams were in the room next to them which had no internal door. Robert and William Jones were stationed at the other side of the building in two adjoining rooms. None of the pairs had open communication with the others. (Eric Thornton)

Note: See appendix for further step-by-step diagrams showing the various movements that took place in the hospital.

The Joneses and Williamses were not paired together by chance. Alphabetically, the Joneses ran consecutively on the company roster held by Colour-Sergeant Bourne. There were five Joneses in the company present that day, with Robert and William being the fourth and fifth alphabetically with that surname owing to the initial of their Christian names.

There were four men of 'B' Company at Rorke's Drift with the surname of Williams. The names of John Williams and Joseph Williams were also placed one after the other alphabetically. It is too much of a coincidence to suggested that these men were chosen randomly by Bourne.

As the designated cook for the hospital, Henry Hook knew the patients and the layout of the building and therefore was perfectly placed to defend it. The reason behind the selection of Thomas Cole, is not known. Perhaps he was selected at random.

'The half-dozen of us who had been told off to defend the hospital were put in corners where we could shoot best through loopholes' related Hook.'[28]

Preparations were still ongoing when at approximately 16:30, Fred Hitch, who had been stationed on the storehouse roof as look-out, shouted down that the Zulus had arrived. As they came into view, the men steadied themselves in readiness for what they knew would be the toughest fight of their lives.

4

THE ZULUS ATTACK

The veteran Undi Corps of the Zulu Impi attacked from the flank of the Oscarsberg. Having been held in reserve for the attack at iSandlwana they had been frustrated by their lack of action and had crossed the river seeking trouble. Four regiments would attack Rorke's Drift, totalling perhaps 3000-4000 warriors. The iNdluyengwe were the first to attack. Charging at the south wall of the mission station, 500 warriors surged towards the post. The hospital lay directly in front of them.

At one of the loopholes, Henry Hook took aim:

> The Zulus once in sight of the station, immediately divided into two columns, advancing at an acute angle, taking advantage of the multitude of huge ant-hills, four or five feet high, and of the dry gullies that had served as water-courses in the rainy season, to shelter themselves. We let them come on until within six hundred yards, and we gave them a volley which brought down a few and drove some back; but the others continued dashing forward, bounding overt the ground, leaping six feet in the air, amid deafening shrieks and yells.[29]

Hook was a renowned shot and 'was able to clip more than one Zulu at a good distance...'[30]

But still they came on:

> The Zulus came on at a wild rush, and although many of them were shot down, they got within about fifty yards of our south wall of mealie-bags, biscuit boxes and waggons. They were caught between two fires–that from the hospital and that from the storehouse–and were checked; but they gained the shelter of

the depot cookhouse and ovens and gave us many heavy volleys.[31]

For Hook, the next stage of the battle would consist of an exchange of fire with those who had taken cover to his front as well as others who had made their way onto the Oscarsberg to fire down on the defence.

Illustration from the *Royal Magazine*, 1905 depicting Hook in his corner room with the only patient in there–a friendly native belonging to the NNC who had sustained assegai wounds to the leg during the fighting at Sihayo's homestead.

Meanwhile, the bulk of the Zulus swung round the hospital towards the front of the building and hurled themselves against the barricades. This was a precarious position, not least because the barricade was incomplete, and a multitude of bushes, shrubs and trees together with a brick wall provided the Zulus with an abundance of cover from which to launch their assaults from short-range. This area would see some of the heaviest fighting and Bromhead personally led this hand-to-hand struggle, but with men like Fred Hitch, Ferdinand Schiess, and James Dalton alongside him, he was in very good company.

A number of able-bodied patients has also taken position outside at the front of the hospital. At some point early in the fight, Thomas Cole informed Hook that he was not staying and left to fight at the barricades in front of the building. Hook couldn't have been too happy about this as it left him with two loopholes to man. The reason for Cole's departure has never come to light. Donald Morris in his book, *The Washing of the Spears,* stated that Cole suffered from claustrophobia and that 'after a while he could stand the confinement no longer and fled…'[32]

In his narrative, Morris wrote that this occurred before the Zulus attacked, when the barricades were still being formed. There is no evidence to suggest that Cole suffered from claustrophobia. Had he been known to have had this condition, surely he would not have been chosen to defend the building in the first place. Additionally, it is clear from the accounts from those who were there that Morris was mistaken and Cole didn't leave until the battle was underway. At any rate, Cole's battle would soon be over. Outside, he would be shot in the head by a Zulu gunman and killed.

Hook would've had no idea what was happening at any part of the defence other than his own. His small, dark, and stuffy room, filled with the smoke from the rapid firing of his Martini-Henry rifle, together with the screams of the native patient did little to improve Hook's mood.

Behind the iNdluyengwe came three more regiments, the uThulwana, the uDloko, and the iNdlondlo, that followed their route around the hospital to the front of the mission station.

Hook was still busy plugging away:

I recollect particularly one Zulu. He was about 400 yards off, and was running from one anthill to another. As he was running from cover to cover, I fired at him; my bullet caught him in the body, and he made a complete somersault. Another man was lying below an anthill, about 300 yards off popping his head out now and again to fire. I took careful aim, but my bullet went just over his head. I then lowered my sight, and fired again the next time he showed himself. I saw the bullet strike the ground in a direct line, but about ten yards short. I then took a little fuller sight, aimed at the spot where I knew his head would come out, and, when he never showed himself again.'[33]

Next door to Hook, the patients who could hold a rifle were also firing at any target that presented itself. At the opposite end of the hospital, William Jones and Robert Jones were doing the same.

At some point, after his rifle began to jam, Hook moved out of his corner room into the neighbouring room which held around nine patients. Despite the native's pleas to be taken with him, Hook left the native behind in the corner room. 'I retired by a partition door into the next room,' recalled Hook. 'For a few minutes I was the only fighting man there. A wounded man of the 24th came to me from another room with a bullet wound in the arm. I tied it up.'[34]

This man can only be Private John Waters, 1/24th, who was the only man in the building at the time whose wound tallies with Hook's description.

Waters was a hospital orderly serving under Surgeon Reynolds and since he belonged to another battalion Hook may not have known him by name.

By now Hook might have been told about the situation outside, more specifically what had occurred in front of the hospital. Waters had been defending the front of the building, so it is distinctly possible that he informed Hook of the developments. He couldn't have been too pleased to discover that the barricades in front of the hospital had been lost and that the defenders had been forced to retire to a makeshift dog-leg barricade that had been hastily thrown up.

The only thing now stopping the Zulus from forcing their way in through the front door was Bromhead and a few men that he had gathered to counter the threat. Every time the Zulus charged the front door of the hospital, Bromhead would charge out from behind the dog-leg to clear them away at the point of the bayonet. Bromhead did this many times, much to the relief and appreciation of the men inside who were desperately holding the front of the building which had the only unbarricaded external door. Unfortunately, developments would lead to these bayonet charges ceasing when the defenders outside condensed their position further by giving up the main yard owing to pressure from the Zulu attacks along the main wall.

Lieutenant Bromhead leads a handful of defenders in a bayonet charge to clear the front of the hospital in order to prevent them forcing an entry into the hospital. He would carry out multiple charges in his efforts to protect the sick and wounded inside the building. (Artist: Steve Noon, commissioned by the author)

After having his wound bound up, Private Waters returned to the front of the building. Not long after this, John Williams came bursting through the internal door to Hook, 'and above the din of battle and of the cries of the wounded', he shouted: 'The Zulus are swarming all over the place! They've dragged Joseph Williams out and killed him!'[35]

This was startling news indeed. Until now, Hook had not engaged in hand-to-hand combat. The Zulus hadn't breached the door in his corner room, and the front was still somehow holding out. But this latest development was the turning point.

***

John and Joseph Williams had the misfortune of holding the worst spot of the entire defence. Perhaps more unfortunate were the patients in this room who were in no state to take part in the defence. All they could do was lie and wait and hope that their protectors would hold off the scores of Zulus swarming around the building.

No doubt because he was a patient and not allocated to defend the hospital, and perhaps because he belonged to the 1/24th and not the

22

2/24th, the fact that Private William Horrigan took an active part in the hand-to-hand fight in this room and did as much as the Williamses, is often overlooked.

Horrigan defended the enclosed room with the Williamses. The room did not have an internal door connecting it to any other part of the building and the only door was external which opened into the Zulus who made determined efforts to batter the door down and force an entrance. When they succeeded, both Joseph Williams and Horrigan went down fighting. Together with Private Garret Hayden who was in no condition to fight, they were dragged outside and cut to pieces before their comrade's eyes. The killing of these men temporarily distracted the Zulus which provided John Williams with the opportunity to mouse-hole through the internal wall. Making his escape, he brought two patients with him into Hook's room.

'What were we to do?' said Hook, 'We were pinned like rats in a hole.'[36] From here, the situation in the hospital rapidly declined. The Zulus were forcing the barricaded outer door in Hook's original corner room, the door into the room held by the Williamses had already been breached, and the defence at the front of the building was crumbling with the men there making individual dashes for liberty when the chance arose. Things outside were also going from bad to worse, the men falling back from the main yard to the biscuit box retrenchment barricade where they were still under heavy attack. Hook and the men with him had no way of knowing this, but the hospital had been essentially abandoned, and friendly troops on the outside were now out of contact with it, the empty yards separating them from their comrades.

Worse still. A thick heavy smoke would soon begin to rise from the hospital's roof. With resistance diminishing, somewhere along the west-end of the building, the Zulus had managed to set the thatch on fire.

Hook yelled at Williams to grab the pick that had been used to make the loopholes and to start breaking through the wall into the next room running along the rear of the building. 'Whilst he was doing this,' noted Hook, 'the Zulus beat the door in, and tried to enter. I stood at the side and shot and bayoneted several–I could not tell how many, but there were five or six lying at my feet.'[37]

The Zulus, it seems, had broken in through the external door of his original corner room, but Hook killed every opponent that faced him.

One had grabbed his rifle and tried to pull it away, but Hook had managed to reload and shoot the Zulu at point-blank range. The attacks continued, but the Zulus could only attack him one at a time. 'Time after time again the Zulus gripped the muzzle and tried to tear the rifle from my grasp, and time after time I wrenched it back. Because I had a better grip than they had.'[38]

Illustrations showing Hook defending the hospital doorway against multiple attackers.

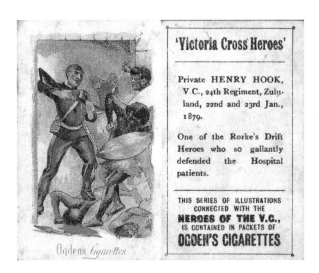

The front and reverse of an Ogden's cigarette card showing Hook standing firm at the door in the hospital.

Hook defends the doorway into his original corner room during the fighting in the hospital. (Artist: Jason Askew, commissioned by the author)

Assegais were thrown at Hook continually, but only one touched him inflicting a scalp wound which he took little notice of at the time. It was a lucky escape and could have been much worse had he not been wearing his helmet which took the brunt of it.

By now Hook described fighting 'over the soles of my boots in blood'.[39]

> I felt I should not be able to stand it much longer. For a space I defended the threshold with my bayonet, husbanding the few cartridges I had left, and at every lull in the enemy's frantic onslaughts I piled corpse upon corpse in the doorway before me, along with anything else I could lay my hands on until I had formed a solid breastwork reaching my shoulders.[40]

By now the friendly native in the corner room was dead, the Zulus having killed him after asking some questions. Hook had heard the Zulus speaking with him and described the native attempting to tear his bandages off and escape.

During one lull, Hook had peered back into the room to find a young

Zulu making off with his kit. Smashing the stock of his rifle down on the lad's head, Hook 'not only smashed the Zulus skull', but also smashed the stock of his rifle 'all to pieces.'[41] A short time after, when the young Zulu began to stir and flicker his eyes, Hook had blown his brains out.

Hook's make-shift barricade made things slightly easier and soon, Williams was through the first wall into the next room–a small stockroom–which was unmanned with no internal doors, and one external door which had been barricaded from the outside. When preparations to defend the building were ongoing, it had been decided that there would be little point in stationing men in there. Anybody in the room would be completely isolated with nowhere to go and targets facing that wall were already well covered from the other larger rooms either side.

Williams assisted the patients through the gap in the wall until there was just one man remaining, Private John Connolly from 'C' Company, 2/24th, who was completely immobile. It was no coincidence that Williams had left Connolly for Hook to move. Connolly had fallen from a wagon some days earlier and had been left hanging upside down, his legs in the air and his kneecap ripped out of its socket. The slightest movement caused him intense agony.

From the doorway Hook glanced back at Connolly and the small hole in the wall. He could hear Williams smashing through the next wall which would bring them into the rooms where the Joneses and another group of patients were located. Connolly begged for Hook not to leave him. Picking his moment, Hook dashed from the doorway, yanked him from his bed and dragged him through the hole. Connolly screamed in agony and Hook thought he'd broken Connolly's leg again. As soon as they'd got through, the Zulus charged into the empty room 'with furious cries of disappointment and rage.'[42]

> Now there was a repetition of the work of holding the doorway, except that I had to stand by a hole, instead of a door while Williams picked away at the far wall to make an opening for escape into the next room. There was more desperate and almost hopeless fighting, as it seemed; but most of the poor fellows were got through the hole. Again, I had to drag Conley [sic] through, a terrific task, because he was a very heavy man.[43]

Here Hook's description is somewhat vague. Around this time at least one man was killed, yet Hook, without elaborating, simply says that 'most' got through.

As he broke through the next wall, Williams would have noticed almost immediately that the end rooms had already seen some serious fighting. The external door to his right had been breached and dead Zulus lay sprawled about the place. The body of Sergeant Maxfield lay in the room, pierced by multiple assegai wounds. But no living soul remained. The Joneses and their patients had vanished.

Private John Williams, who broke through the partition walls in the hospital.

***

William Jones and Robert Jones had held the south-east corner of the hospital since the start of the battle. They had fired countless shots at the Zulus as they launched their first attack and had kept up a steady fire at targets ever since. A window high up on the gable wall overlooking the yard allowed them to keep in touch with the men in the yard outside. At some point they became aware that the defenders had condensed their perimeter by giving up the yard and peeling back to take up a position behind the biscuit box barricade. They had shouted for and received extra ammunition courtesy of Surgeon Reynolds who at great risk to his life had dashed across the abandoned yard to throw some packets up to them.

Hook and the others with him in the hospital had no open communication with the Joneses and were not aware of any developments outside of their own small space. They knew nothing of the Joneses defending their outer door against furious Zulu assaults, nor of their urgent evacuation from the gable window after the Zulus had breached their door. The Joneses had managed to save all but one patient under their care, the delirious Sergeant Maxfield being the unfortunate exception.

It must have come as a huge surprise for John Williams when he broke through to their room to find it empty. But no time could be wasted. It was clear which way the men previously holding the room had gone—the window being their obvious escape route. Williams and the patients struggled through. In no time at all, men were dropping from the window into the empty yard. Finding themselves in no-man's-land, they quickly gathered their bearings and made their way to the new position where the defenders were still holding out.

At this point, Hook and Connolly were alone in the hospital, Williams having followed the other patients out. Quite how Hook managed to get Connolly to safety isn't known for certain since the primary accounts differ in their finer detail. One account from 1898 stated that Hook, presumably after they were clear of the building, 'managed to hoist the broken-legged man on to his back.'[44]

Connolly, however, in a statement shortly after the battle, wrote that he climbed out of the window 'by placing mealie bags...

> ...and made for the bush by sitting down and pushing myself along feet first. After going 50 yards I got into the bush and laid down to keep out of sight.
> The hospital was set on fire at 7.45. The Zulus kept passing me all night, but either did not see me or thought me dead.
> Our own men kept firing into the bush till 4a.m. from a distance of 150 yards, but I was not hit by any bullet.
> About 5 a.m. on the 23rd, I crawled back into the entrenchment...[45]

Surgeon Reynolds supported the theory of Hook and Connolly exiting by other means rather than the window that would have dropped them into the yard, when he said:

Private Hook, 2/24th Regiment, who was acting hospital cook, and Private Connolly, 2/24th Regiment, a patient in hospital, made their way into the open at the back of the hospital, by breaking a hole in the wall with a pickaxe then climbing over the sacks into the curtailed laager.[46]

To add to the confusion, Connolly, in 1887 in reply to a series of questions, completely contradicted his earlier account by saying he was helped 'out through a window, and I crawled in a sitting posture backwards towards the barn [storehouse].'[47]

Upon being asked if he reached the 'barn' safely, Connolly, again, in contradiction to his earlier account where he stated he remained hidden in the bushes all night, answered that he did and went on to describe taking an active part in the defence from the storehouse, firing his rifle from a loophole throughout the night.

In both of his accounts, Connolly insisted he crawled the distance. Yet Hook's version changed little over the years, and he remained adamant that he had carried Connolly. In describing Hook's actions following their exit from the building, an account of Hook's from *Macmillian's Magazine*, noted that Connolly was 'tall, and, powerless to help himself, [and] hung like a sack, his feet dragging along the ground':

The slow progress was frightful. An assegai hurled through the air struck the man, but fortunately stuck harmlessly in his over-coat. Great beads of sweat gathered on Hook's brow; his veins stood out like cords; his breath came in broken grasps; his legs tottered beneath him. One more supreme effort and he neared the barricade; he was seen, recognised and helped inside, both rescuer and rescued unharmed by spear or bullet.[48]

Hook undoubtedly dragged Connolly through the hospital and saved his life, but due to the discrepancies above, it is impossible to know precisely how they reached the inner compound.

Whatever happened, Hook and Connolly were the last two men to leave the building. Once they had made their escape, the battle for the hospital was over.

'The Defence of Rorke's Drift' showing a variety of those who took part in the battle, including Lieutenants Chard and Bromhead (centre), and the wounded Fred Hitch (right) carrying ammunition. (Artist: Lady Butler)

Another famous depiction of the battle. Lieutenant Bromhead stands in the centre pointing. Reverend Smith hands out ammunition to his right, whilst Lieutenant Chard stands at the barricades (far right) accepting ammunition from a wounded comrade. (Artist: Alphonse de Neuville)

A close-up of de Neuville's painting showing the evacuation from the
hospital. The painting inaccurately depicts the barricades around the
hospital still being held by the defenders but in reality, the evacuation took
place across a no-man's-land with the men from the building having to run
across the abandoned yard to reach their comrades outside. Hook is
thought to be the man carrying an injured comrade (Connolly) on his back.
(Artist: Alphonse de Neuville)

Hook had started the battle with 100 rounds in his pouch and stuffed
about his person. By the time he exited the hospital they had all but
gone. Williams had just two bullets remaining when he left the hospital.
After replenishing his stock, Hook slotted in with his comrades at the
barricades. He was ordered to hold a position on the biscuit box
barricade facing the hospital where 'three men had just been hit.'[49] One
of these men, Corporal Jack Lyons who had been shot in the neck, lay
where he fell, unable to be moved. Throughout the night he would
continuously cry out in agony and regularly ask Hook to move his head
from one side to the other to ease his pain. Corporal Allen had also
been shot in the arm here but was able to keep himself busy
distributing ammunition to the defenders. The third man to be hit at

Hook's spot may have been James Langley Dalton, whose apparent fearlessness would earn him the everlasting respect of the men of the 24th. He was shot through the shoulder whilst fighting from the biscuit box retrenchment but remained on his feet to cheer and encourage the men.

Earlier in the battle the position in front of the hospital had been lost and the defenders had retired to the dog-leg barricade. The Zulus had then extended their attacks along the whole north wall and more than once had come close to breaking in and overrunning the entire position. Chard had then made the decision to withdraw from the main yard area, a crucial move credited with saving the entire defence from being overwhelmed and wiped out. Now, from the storehouse compound, they were able to withstand the Zulu attacks, although casualties would continue to mount. Fred Hitch received a bullet to his shoulder which shattered the bone whilst he was fighting from a precarious corner sector which was open to attack from multiple angles. Corporal Ferdinand Schiess, NNC, had also been wounded here, as had Lance-Sergeant Williams whose wounds would prove fatal. Almost all casualties occurred at the deadly corner section where the biscuit box wall met the north wall, and along the biscuit box barricade itself, where Hook was now posted.

Zulu attacks continued against the north wall, particularly the corner section. The Zulus did not attempt to charge the biscuit box retrenchment, but they remained hotly engaged in exchanges of fire.

In the darkness, the fire from the now blazing hospital thatch illuminated the abandoned yard to the defender's advantage. Therefore, the Zulus switched their attention to the opposite side of the defence by the storehouse and stone cattle enclosure (kraal). Determined attempts to set the storehouse roof alight failed.

Chard made a few more tactical adjustments to improve the defence. The cattle kraal was abandoned in two stages, but not before a large redoubt of mealie bags had been formed within the defensive area in which marksmen were placed as well as some of the wounded.

Enemy attacks stagnated, but the Zulus kept up a steady fire on the position which eventually dwindled as the night wore on. In the early hours when all was quiet it was deemed safe for the watercart that had been left in the yard near the hospital to be retrieved to provide water for the wounded. Hook, who was directly facing the cart, was one of several men who went out and dragged it in.

The retrieval of the watercart is often described as a 'charge', or 'bayonet charge', but this is a misconception. The Zulus were not active at this point, and the cart was collected without Zulu interference, as stated by Hook in more than one account. In fact, according to Hook, the Zulus had already retired from the immediate area:

> About 3a.m. day began to break, and the Zulus retreated. A party, of which I was one, then volunteered to go across to the hospital, where there was a water cart, and bring it in to the inner enclosure, where there was no water, and the wounded were crying for it.[50]

As the sun rose, the defenders were relieved to see the Zulus had retired and were no longer surrounding the position. At first, the men peered cautiously over the barricades, then they stood in full view. Still, no shots came.

The defenders ventured out from the safety of their defence to look for their missing comrades. Hook found one man, 'kneeling behind the outer defences with his rifle to his shoulder, and resting on the parapet as if he were taking aim.'[51] Hook touched the man's shoulder and suggested he come back to the inner defences. It wasn't until the man slumped to the side that Hook realised he was dead. The hospital–the thatch of which had now burnt itself out–was the main focus of the search. Miraculously, several patients, after fleeing the hospital mid-battle, had remained hidden outside the perimeter throughout the night and came in safely. But most of the missing men were dead. Hook saw several of them mutilated around the hospital. Inside he looked at the body of Sergeant Maxfield which was now heavily burnt.

Within the hospital, Hook described seeing 'the charred remains of our slaughtered comrades amid the heap of smoking rubbish':

> Hard by lay the bodies of other brave fellows, all assegaied and mutilated in a most shocking fashion. Around, for hundreds of yards, the ground was strewn with the ebony corpses of the ferocious savages we had laid low with our rifles during the afternoon and night, along with firearms and assegais presenting steel heads of various forms steeped in gore. Those having crescent-shaped blades were the most terrible among the

weapons of this description that we had to fight against. A wound from one of them, when it had been twisted round and withdrawn, proved inevitably mortal, and brought death amid atrocious agony. There was also a quantity of guns.[52]

Curiosity got the better of Hook and he wandered out by himself to see if he could see the body of the Zulu who had taken cover behind the ant hill early in the battle. Hook had taken three shots at him and after the third the Zulu hadn't showed himself again. Walking to the spot, Hook was pleased to find that his final shot had struck the Zulu through the head.

Going on a little further into a gully, Hook noticed an apparently dead Zulu, bleeding from the leg. He found it strange that a dead man was still freely bleeding, and tried to cautiously walk by:

I was passing him by when he made a yell and clutched the butt of my rifle, dragging himself on to his knees. We had a severe struggle which lasted for several seconds, when finding he could not get the rifle from me, he let go with one hand and caught me round the leg, trying to throw me. Whilst he was doing this I got the rifle from him, and drawing back a yard or two, loaded and blew his brains out.[53]

Other soldiers had witnessed Hook's struggle, so too had the officers, who summoned everyone back behind the barricades and issued orders that no one was to leave the perimeter unless in a group. Hook then went out with several comrades and carried in some wounded Zulus.

Even the cheeriest defenders were feeling the stresses of their ordeal. 'But we had no time to dwell on the awful scene about us,' noted Hook:

We did not know how sooner another assault might be made, but we did know that if the Zulus kept on attacking us it was only a question of time before we were cut to pieces, as our comrades a dozen miles away had been destroyed.

The roof of the hospital had fallen in by this time, and only the storehouse was standing. We were ordered to put ropes through the loopholes of the walls of the hospital, and pull them down. This we did, and the walls, which had already been weakened by our picks, partially collapsed. Then we tore away the thatch from the storehouse, so that the Zulus could not, even if they wished, set fire to it, as they had fired the hospital. With the ruins of the walls we strengthened our little fort, and again waited for the Zulus–if they cared to come.[54]

Somewhere between 8-9am, their worst fears came true when the Zulus reappeared on a nearby hill and began to edge closer as if to attack. The men rushed to their posts and prepared for battle, but the Zulus hesitated and did not commit to an assault. From their position on the hill, they could see something that the defenders could not.

After spending the night at iSandlwana amongst their dead comrades, Lord Chelmsford and his portion of the column were now marching towards Rorke's Drift. Faced with this new threat, the exhausted Zulus backed away and retired from the field.

The British column was in no mood to fight. Luckily, neither were the Zulus, and the two forces passed each other, content to leave any further fighting for another day.

The column arrived at the station to loud cheers. Hook immediately reverted to his job of hospital cook. By now the hospital was a smouldering wreck, but the patients still needed tending to, and that was Hook's main priority. In his 'shirt-sleeves' with his braces hanging down loose, Hook began cooking and making tea for the sick and wounded.

Lord Chelmsford, after congratulating the men for their successful defence, pulled Chard and Bromhead to one side to hear their account of the battle. Surrounded by his staff and officers of the regiment, Chelmsford had heard all about the fight for the hospital and the rescue of the patients.

Hook was still cooking when a sergeant ran up and told him that Lieutenant Bromhead wanted to see him immediately. Hook went to put his coat on, but the sergeant insisted he came at once. He nervously did so, thinking he had committed some sort of offence and was in trouble. But he needn't have worried. 'I went into the midst of the officers,' recalled Hook, 'and Lord Chelmsford asked me all about the defence of the hospital, as I was the last to leave the building.'[55]

Hook admitted that he was so nervous and worn out from the day's events that he mumbled his way through it and didn't make much sense when explaining what he had done. Nevertheless, after hearing

Hook's description, Chelmsford praised him for his bravery, shook him by the hand, and told him he would always be there if he needed anything. Also present was Captain Penn Symons, 2/24th, who jotted down the names of those who had defended the hospital, with information on what each of them had done. He would later write a full and detailed account of the battle after speaking with many of the defenders who took part.

Even at this early stage it seems that Lord Chelmsford had certain men in mind for the Victoria Cross. Certainly, this was the case a little later in the day when he spoke with the severely wounded Fred Hitch who had been unconscious when the column had arrived. Bending down to the wounded private, Chelmsford told Hitch that Bromhead have provided an account of his bravery. 'I will recommend you for the V.C.,' he informed Hitch, 'and if you only survive, you may be sure I will do everything that lies in my power for you.'[56]

Lord Chelmsford (Ron Sheeley)

Although Hook knew of a man in the battalion, William Griffiths, who already had a Victoria Cross, he later admitted that he 'didn't really know or care for the VC before he got one.'[57]

***

An account from Commandant 'Maori' Hamilton Browne, NNC, who was a part of Lord Chelmsford's force, described the scene at Rorke's Drift as they found it when they arrived:

> The dead Zulus lay in piles, in some places as high as the top of the parapet... The attack must have been well pushed home and both sides deserve the greatest credit. The hospital was still smouldering and the stench from the burning flesh of the dead inside was very bad... Some of our sick and wounded had been burned inside of the hospital and a number of Zulus had been also killed inside of the building itself. In front of the hospital lay a large number of Zulus also a few of our men, who had been patients, and who when the hospital had been set on fire had, in trying to escape, rushed out among the enemy and been killed, their bodies being also ripped open and mutilated.[58]

After the battle, a major clean-up operation took place. Some wounded Zulus were killed, and the dead were collected. 'As for our own comrades,' noted Hook, 'we, who had fought side by side with them, buried them':

> This was done the day after the fight, not far from the place where they fell, and at the foot of the hill. Soon afterwards, a little cemetery was walled in and a monument was put up in the middle. The lettering was cut on it by a very clever bandsman named Mellsop, who used bits of broken bayonets as chisels. He drew a capital picture of the fight. Those who had been killed in action were buried on one side of the cemetery, and those who died of disease on the other side.[59]

For reasons unknown, Storekeeper Byrne was buried outside the cemetery walls. Hook didn't know why but speculated that it may have been because he wasn't a regular soldier. Byrne had been shot in the head whilst giving a drink to a wounded man by the barricades. A harsh decision, if Hook is correct.

Fifteen defenders were killed at Rorke's Drift, and a further two– Lance-Sergeant Williams and Private William Beckett (or Becket)–died from their wounds. The number of wounded was higher than the official tally. Men had been hit and badly bruised by spent balls from

Zulu gunfire and suffered a number of minor injuries and wounds that went unreported at the time. Hook didn't bother to have his scalp wound seen to and as such does not feature on the official list of wounded.

Whilst Zulu casualties are unknown, 351 bodies that were collected from the immediate area were buried in a mass grave. A number of wounded and worn-out Zulus were killed in the fields around the station after the battle, and many others would have retired with various wounds. Many other dead bodies were scattered around the post and their remains were still being found months later. Without doubt, Zulus casualties were extremely high.

5

HOOK LEAVES THE ARMY

For the soldiers at Rorke's Drift, their time spent at the mission station after the battle was a terrible experience, fraught with sickness and discomfort. To counter the bitter cold, Hook cut holes in a mealie bag and wore it to try to keep warm. Yet his letters home to his parents 'made no allusions to any serious hardships', nor did Hook tell them what he had done during the battle, his aim being not to cause any worry.[60]

Shortly after his arrival, Lord Chelmsford rode on to Helpmekaar, and by the 26 January was in Pietermaritzburg to pick up the pieces of the recent defeat. Free from the shackles of Lord Chelmsford's presence, Colonel Glyn, who was grieving considerably from the loss of his battalion at iSandlwana, banned anyone from venturing from the now strengthened mission station.

Photograph of the storehouse at Rorke's Drift, taken from inside the perimeter (named 'Fort Bromhead' after the battle) with the Shiyane hill in the background. As can be seen, the position was built up and strengthened in case of further Zulu attack. The thatch was removed on 23 January due to Zulu efforts to set it alight during the battle.

There was a constant heavy rain, and with hundreds of men now squeezed into one small area, the ground soon became a quagmire. Typhoid fever and dysentery were rife, and swarms of flies made even the simplest of jobs impossible. Due to their heroic defence, 'B' Company, 2/24th, were granted the honour of sleeping in the attic of the now thatchless storehouse with a tarpaulin to prevent them from the elements.

Some restructuring took place and on 29 January Hook was transferred from 'B' Company to 'G' Company. Later, on 3 April, he would be detached from 'G' Company and moved to 'E' Company.

Amongst those killed at iSandlwana was Major Black's servant. Black needed a replacement, and Hook–a model soldier and soon-to-be recipient of the Victoria Cross–fit the bill perfectly. The role would bring Hook extra pay, 'one shilling and sixpence in the infantry, but usually more is given'.[61]

Hook evidently enjoyed his new role and in a letter home he told his mother that Major Black was 'a nice gentleman' and that he 'liked him very much'.[62]

The appointment garnered some laughs too. Major Black was an exceptional soldier and something of a character. He was a Glaswegian and is described as having a shrill voice with a broad Scotch accent. Black's voice could often be heard at Rorke's Drift as he called out for Hook at the top of his lungs. 'So the men had their little joke', recalled Captain Harford, 'and whenever Hook was called for they themselves shouted for Hook and then yelled out, "I think he's hooked it, sir!", which always caused great merriment.'[63]

Lieutenant Bromhead did not like talking about Rorke's Drift. A quiet, modest man who wrote home describing his sorrow at the loss of his men and the way in which they had been killed, he showed little enthusiasm when asked by Chelmsford's staff to compile a report on the battle. But evidence exists to suggest that he did eventually submit a report with the help of a friend, possibly Captain Penn Symons.

This report has either never surfaced or was not a 'report' as such but Bromhead's official letter of recommendation to members of his company who had distinguished themselves. Addressed to 'The Officer Commanding 2/24th Regt,' and dated 15 February 1879, Bromhead's statement reads:

I beg to bring to your notice the names of the following men belonging to my Company who especially distinguished themselves during the attack by the Zulus on this Post on 22nd & 23rd January last; & whose conduct on this occasion came under my personal cognizance.

No. 1395 Private John Williams was posted by me together with Private Joseph Williams & Private William Horrigan 1/24th Regt. in a further room of the Hospital. They held it for more than an hour, so long as they had a round of ammunition left, when, as communication was for the time cut off, the Zulus were enabled to advance & burst open the door. They dragged out Private Joseph Williams & two of the patients by the arms, & assegaied them. Whilst the Zulus were occupied with the slaughter of these unfortunate men, a lull took place, during which Private John Williams–who with two patients were the only men now left alive in this ward–succeeded in knocking a hole in the partition, & in taking the two patients with him into the next ward, where he found

No. 1373 Private Henry Hook. These two men together, one man working whilst the other fought & held the enemy at bay with his bayonet, broke through three more partitions, & were thus enabled to bring eight patients through a small window into our inner line of defence.

In another ward, facing the hill, I had placed

No. 593 Private William Jones & No. 716 Private Robert Jones: They defended their post to the last, until six out of the seven patients it contained had been removed. The seventh, Sergeant Maxfield, 2/24th Regt: was delirious with fever. Although they had previously dressed him, they were unable to induce him to move. When Private Robert Jones returned to endeavour to carry him away, he found him being stabbed by the Zulus as he lay on his bed.'[64]

Bromhead went on to write up the actions of Corporal Allen and Private Hitch outside the hospital when providing covering fire from an exposed position for the patients who were crossing the yard, after which, when wounded, they had supplied their comrades with ammunition.

Upon receipt of Bromhead's report, his commanding officer, Lieutenant-Colonel Degacher forwarded it to column commander,

Colonel Glyn, 'in the hope that the conspicuous gallantry of the men named in the margin and mentioned in Lt. Bromhead's letter, may be brought by H.R.H. the Commander-in-Chief to the notice of Her Majesty the Queen, and be deemed worthy of the Victoria Cross being awarded to them'.[65]

Ultimately, all of these recommendations would be successful, and the men awarded the Victoria Cross. In time, more from other units would follow; a total of eleven would be awarded for the battle.[66]

When Penn Symons compiled his extensive account on the battle after speaking with the defenders directly, Bromhead's recommendations would be included almost word for word into the account, the original of which is held in the Royal Welsh Military Museum in Brecon. It is probable that Penn Symons played a major part in writing Bromhead's report.

The citations for the Rorke's Drift Victoria Crosses would also be virtually identical in wording to Bromhead's report of their bravery.

Hook received his VC on 3 August 1879 by Fort Melvill–a fort that had been constructed on the high ground overlooking the ponts by the river–'not much than 600 yards from the spot where the hospital stood.'[67] By this time, a successful second invasion of Zululand had taken place, and the war was over. The VC was presented by Sir Garnet Wolseley who had replaced Lord Chelmsford as Commander-in-Chief:

Punctually the men were drawn up, and Sir Garnet, attended by Gen. Colley, Col. Brackenbury and Capt. Braithwaite rode up, with Col. East and Capt. Stewart–Col. Degacher, Lieut. Col. Black, Capt. Church, and Lieuts. Logan and Lloyd being the 24th officers present. A general salute was given, and then the warrant was read out referring to the occasion and bestowal of the decoration; after which Sir Garnet said: 'Colonel Degacher, officers and men of the 24th Regiment,–It is always a very great pleasure to a General Officer to give away such a decoration as the Victoria Cross; but the pleasure on this occasion was doubled, as he was able to present it on the spot where the deed for which it was given was performed. The defence of Rorke's Drift would always be remembered in future history, and especially in that of the regiment, in which no act would ever appear which was braver, or the memory of which would be more cherished, than the Defence of Rorke's Drift, on January

22nd, 1879.' The cross having been handed to the General by Colonel Brackenbury, and Private Hook called up, His Excellency pinned it on his breast himself. This concluded the ceremony, after which Sir Garnet rode down the lines, and the men were then dismissed. The man, who is quite a young fellow, was much congratulated by his officers and fellow-soldiers ... During the day Sir Garnett and his Staff went over the scene of the brilliant defence, and then remained quietly in camp all day.[68]

Three months after his arrival in South Africa back in 1878, Hook had joined the Good Templars at Pietermaritzburg and had taken the pledge not to drink alcohol as long as he remained in the country. Yet he admitted, 'I was sorely tempted to break the pledge the day I got the cross, even the officers offered me a drink, but I firmly refused; I had not even been in the habit of drinking my allowance of rum; I gave that away.'[69]

Hook may have resisted the temptation of a drink to celebrate his VC, but a subsequent account published in the *Natal Witness*, suggests he may have strayed from his pledge directly after the battle itself. 'He was a teetotaller at the time," reported the newspaper, 'and after the black hordes had been shot down, and the remaining numbers had retired to a safe distance, Hook was asked by the Sergeant if he would take a nip, and replied, 'I think I will after that lot!'[70]

It is difficult to imagine what was going through Wolseley's mind as he presented Hook with his Victoria Cross. Privately he was very critical of the Rorke's Drift awards and also of the recognition that Lieutenants Melvill and Coghill were receiving for attempting to save the 1/24th's Queen's Colour following the collapse of the iSandlwana camp.[71] After presenting Hook with his VC, Wolseley wrote scathing remarks in his personal journal claiming it was 'monstrous making heroes... out of those who shut up in the buildings at Roorke's [sic] drift could not bolt & fought like rats for their lives which they could not otherwise save'.[72]

Ironically, years later, when giving his own version of the battle, Hook would describe his predicament in similar terms by saying 'we were pinned like rats in a hole.'[73]

Two images of Hook following the award of his Victoria Cross. The left-hand photograph was seemingly taken not long after he had received his VC, prior to him receiving his campaign medal. (Left-hand image, Ron Sheeley)

Early in September Wolseley received word that the battalion was to move to Gibraltar. A two-week march to Pietermaritzburg concluded on 14 October, but Major Black and Hook had arrived earlier, ahead of the battalion, and were already on their way to Gibraltar.

The battalion arrived on 12 February 1880 where, for the first time in two years–albeit temporarily–they had a roof over their heads. The battalion's time under harsh conditions at Rorke's Drift had taken its toll on most, and large numbers of men stationed there had been ill with typhoid and dysentery. Some were invalided out of the army whilst others died. Amongst the latter number was John Williams–not to be confused with his namesake John Williams VC who defended the hospital–who died of disease two days after Hook had been presented with his VC.

Hook too was suffering and admitted to feeling 'very ill'.[74] He had signed up for six years' service with the army, but by May 1880, he'd had enough. On 25 June 1880, following the statuary 30-day intervention period stated in Queen's Regulations, Hook purchased his discharge from the army for the sum of £18.75.[75]

Wilsone Black, who at the time was in command of the battalion, signed off Hook's certificate of discharge with the following words: 'His conduct has been very good. Granted the decoration of the Victoria Cross for gallantry at the defence of Rorke's Drift. He is in possession of one Good Conduct Badge.'[76]

Now, after almost two years of active service and participation in two wars, Private Henry Hook VC was going home.

Hook (left) stands with an unidentified corporal from the early 1880's. Photograph taken in London.

6

HOOK RETURNS HOME

There is a well-established yet false myth that Hook's wife had assumed him dead and ran off to remarry whilst he was in South Africa. The myth has existed since the 1960's at least. The following passage dates from 1967 and was published in a British Museum staff magazine: 'The family farm had been sold, and his wife–who apparently believed that he had been killed at Rorke's Drift–had married again and moved from the village.'[77]

Stories such as this have been passed down over the years, but are not accurate. Comfort did not move away, nor did she remarry thinking Hook was dead. Census returns show that they were still married, and that she still lived at their home at Mount Pleasant. The farm story is almost certainly family lore.[78]

What is not in doubt is that Hook's marriage to Comfort prior to him going to war was extremely complicated and strained.

Hook and Comfort had married in 1870. Between the years of 1871 and 1876 they'd had three children. Comfort was described by her youngest daughter as 'very strict', someone who was very difficult to be around, and someone who ruled 'with a rod of iron.'[79]

Comfort's family never liked Hook and things must have been very difficult for him, particularly since, shortly after their marriage, Comfort's parents move in with them as 'Boarders'.[80] Family tradition states that Comfort's parents were of the opinion Hook had married her 'to improve his lot in life' and to get his hands on their farm.[81]

To further complicate matters, evidence suggests that Comfort had been having an affair and Hook had found out. Certainly, he knew about it in 1897 when taking steps to have the marriage dissolved, where it would be stated that Comfort, on a number of occasions between December 1876 and February 1877, committed adultery with a man by the name of William Wedley. Indeed, this may have been the reason why Hook enlisted into the regular army in the first place as it coincides exactly with him joining up in March 1877. It may also be the reason why he never returned to them after his discharge from the army.

Hook's reputation within his wife's family was very poor and it was said that 'as an absent husband and father, Hook dropped to a very low point in his family's esteem.'[82] This was passed down to his children and would be passed to his grandchildren. Within the family he would regularly be referred to as 'a bit of a rogue' and 'a womaniser', and his daughter, Julia's, children and grandchildren were brought up to be ashamed of him.[83]

Julia, however, had next to no memory of her father, who joined the army and left when she was just a young girl, and her own opinion was undoubtedly formed through her mother's influence. The truth of the whole matter has long been lost to history.

Whatever the case, when Hook landed in Britain from South Africa, he headed straight for his parent's home in Monmouth, cementing the fact that he had no intention of returning to his wife and children and that his marriage was effectively over. He arrived in July 1880, completely unexpected and unannounced. Local newspapers, picking up on the return of their hero, published articles about him, raising the point that he was seeking to gain employment.

Ever since Rorke's Drift, Hook had suffered from terrible nightmares and upon his return the newspaper reported 'that for a long time after the Zulu campaign he found it no easy task to sleep, for the recollections of what he had experienced there left a remarkable impression on his memory.'[84]

Hook soon found employment working as a groom for Dr. George Owen Willis who had been the assistant surgeon of the local militia when Hook had been a member. Dr. Willis had probably read the article in the local newspaper stating that Hook was looking for work and offered him the job.

In the December, despite the best efforts of Dr. Willis, Hook's father passed away after contracting typhoid fever and developing double pneumonia.

Over the space of the next year, both Hook and his mother had departed Monmouth separately to start afresh. His mother remarried and settled in Cardiff whilst Hook—at some point in late August-early September—moved to London where he quickly found employment working for William Cubitt & Co., a well-established building firm who employed labourers for their various contracts.

William Cubitt & Co. supplied both materials and manpower throughout London, and Hook was sent as a contractor to the British Museum where he was assigned to 'General Cleaning' under the Clerk of Works. Labourers working at the museum came in two forms–those employed through the contractor, and those employed directly by the museum. There were pros and cons for both since contractors were paid slightly more whereas those employed by the museum enjoyed a secure and permanent job, albeit on a lower wage.

Preferring full and permanent work, Hook took steps to gain employment from the museum directly as a 'duster'. The museum, however, would only take on contractors who were 'well recommended' and in possession of 'the necessary qualifications.'[85] Hook required references and put forward Gonville Bromhead, now a major, who was serving with the regiment in Brecon.

Bromhead's reference was positive and straight to the point: 'I have always found Hook an honest & sober man & that I can strongly recommend him for employment.'[86]

Hook also called on Lord Chelmsford to provide a reference. Chelmsford, who had given Hook his word that he would always be there should he need him, was delighted to provide what was needed.

In a letter dated 25 November 1881, Chelmsford also wrote directly to Hook, stating:

Henry Hook,

Mr Fortescue has written to me regarding your wish to obtain the place of 'Inside Duster' at the British Museum, and it has given me great pleasure to be of some slight service to you by writing in your favour to the Principal Librarian.

The promise I made you at Rorke's Drift I shall be always ready to keep to the best of my ability;–as I never forget those who made such a gallant stand and behaved so nobly on that memorable occasion–

Believe me always
Your well wisher
Chelmsford.[87]

These references, particularly the one supplied by Lord Chelmsford, ensured Hook's application was successful. On 29 November he was interviewed by the Principal Librarian where it became apparent that Hook could not read or write. Nevertheless, on Boxing Day, 1881, Hook began work for his new employer. His pay was 24/- a week, and he would work 11 hours a day, six days a week.

A portrait of Hook from the early 1880's.

Hook would work at the museum for the rest of his working career, but from the start there was somewhere else he'd much rather be. Even before he had started his employment with the British Museum, Hook had made efforts to return to South Africa, having applied 'for admission to the ranks' of the Cape Mounted Riflemen (CMR).[88] The CMR acted as both a police force and military force. They hadn't taken part in the Zulu War, but more recently had fought and suffered some losses in Basutoland. Hook had been notified that he was to attend an interview at the Cape 'Emigration Office' in London but that no travel expenses would be covered, meaning if he was successful, he would have to fund his own passage to South Africa. Whether or not Hook turned up for the interview is not known, but nothing further came of his application.

Hook was evidently keen to continue his military service. In February 1882 he volunteered for the 19th Middlesex (Bloomsbury Rifles) with whom he would serve until 1887 when he joined the 17th Middlesex.

The headquarters of the 19th Middlesex were just a few hundred yards from the museum. Hook was assigned to 'H' Company, known as the British Museum Company owing to the high number of staff members in its ranks. In conjunction with his enlistment, he also joined the British Museum Rifle Association.

As the months rolled by, Hook continued to try to find a way to get to South Africa, even if it meant finding employment away from the military. He confided in Gregory Eccles, a colleague of higher standing at the museum who was an officer in the Bloomsbury Rifles. Eccles wrote to his son in Natal, asking if anything could be done for Hook. In turn, Eccles' son wrote to the editor of the *Natal Mercury*:

7 July

To The Editor of the Natal Mercury

Sir,– Referring to your notice relative to Pte. Hook, V.C. I would like to know if something could not be done for him in Natal, that would be better than the very poor post of 'duster' in the British Museum. Surely Natalians will do something for one of the men to whose courage and devotion they owe so much. My father, who is one of the assistant librarians in the British Museum, speaks most highly of Hook's character, and has several times asked me to try and get him something to do out here; but though I have spoken to several influential people, none of them seemed able to do anything; and seeing the above referred to notice in your paper induced me to write to you to solicit your aid in bringing Hook's case before the public. There is only one thing against him, and that is that he is quite uneducated, being unable to read or write with any facility. Trusting you may be able to do something.–I am, &c.,

W. G. Eccles.[89]

Nothing came of it, and Hook's South Africa dream would never materialise.

Hook was extremely dedicated to the Rifles and enjoyed his time with them immensely. During annual dinner in 1885, Hook—now a corporal–received a silver-headed cane, 'presented to the non-commissioned officer making the highest aggregate of marks for attendance at drill'.[90] That same year he won a medal for '1st Drill Prize.'[91]

Yet, in a letter to the commanding officer, he wrote–or rather got someone to write on his behalf–the following letter:

> If there is a vacancy in the Staff of 19th. M.R.V. of any post in which I can be of service–may I take the liberty of asking to be appointed to the Same as I find my Employment does not allow me of attending to the Company Drills as I should wish.[92]

Hook was not offered a staff job, and in January 1887 he resigned from the unit. Two day later, however, he enrolled as a private soldier in the 17th Middlesex but was soon promoted, first to lance-corporal then to corporal within the space of a few months. He would serve with this unit until 1 November 1890, at which point a hiatus from military service lasting more than five years would ensue.

During this period, Hook tried for various other roles, including an attempt in 1892 to become a Yeoman of the Guard with the support of Chelmsford, Wolseley and Chard (Bromhead having died in India).

After nine years as a duster, Hook also began to take on extra work in the evenings as a substitute 'Umbrella Caretaker'. He was carrying out this temporary role when Lord Wolseley visited him in June 1893. Wolseley at the time was in the latter stages of writing a set of books on the Duke of Marlborough and was visiting the museum to undertake some research. [93] Knowing that Hook worked there, Wolseley requested to see him and was reported to have 'greeted him in a most cordial manner.'[94]

When the regular employee in that position retired in 1894, Hook accepted the role on a permanent basis. With the new job came an extra two shillings a week. One visitor to the museum–a reporter–who met Hook when he was an umbrella attendant, described him as 'a short, broad-shouldered, kindly-looking man'.[95] Another would describe him at standing '5ft. 7in. in his socks, measures 42in, round the chest, and is a rather stout but hale and robust man, with a kindly expression of countenance, and a heavy fair moustache.[96]

Hook's new role came with a uniform on which he wore his medals, including his VC. The above reporter, and everyone who met him couldn't help but notice the bronze distinction pinned to his chest. He enjoyed much attention because of it, and most of his accounts on Rorke's Drift came about through this visible public role.

In April 1896, Hook enrolled into the Royal Fusiliers' 1st Volunteer Battalion, a unit he would serve with until right before his death, with the rank of sergeant and Instructor of Musketry.

Hook, as a sergeant-instructor of Musketry with the 1st Volunteer Battalion, Royal Fusiliers.

Hook had lived alone for almost seventeen years after arriving in London. He was living on Hungerford Road in the Holloway area when he began courting Ada Letitia Taylor who was twelve years his junior. It is believed they met at a smoking concert, possibly one held by the Royal Fusiliers at Fitzroy Square where they had their social events. Around the same time, he joined the Loyal St. James's Lodge of Odd Fellows in the 'North London District' of the Manchester Unity located near his home, which, offered 'provisions against sickness, old age and death.'[97] Perhaps Hook's new relationship influenced his decision to join this society for he must have known his health was not all it should be, and he wouldn't wish to burden Ada if it could be helped.

Although living separate lives, Hook and his wife, Comfort, remained married until February 1897. In 1895, however, this had not deterred Comfort from marrying David Meyrick in a civil ceremony in Gloucester. For this reason, and with mention of Comfort's adultery prior to Hook sailing to South Africa, Hook and Comfort's marriage was finally dissolved.

On 10 April 1897, three months after his divorce from Comfort, Hook and Ada Taylor were married. In February 1899, Ada gave birth to their first daughter, Victoria Catherine (it is probably no coincidence that her initials were 'VC'). Their second daughter, Letitia Jean, was born 11 November 1902.

***

Over the years Hook remained in contact with his fellow Rorke's Drift defenders. In 1897, after learning of the deteriorating health of John Chard who was seriously ill with cancer of the tongue, Hook sent him a letter of sympathy. Although Chard read it, he was too poorly to respond. Chard's brother replied, telling Hook that Chard was 'proud to think that the gallant men of the 24th who stood by him at Rorke's Drift have not forgotten him.'[98] Chard's brother went on to inform Hook that he was sorry to say that Chard's condition was hopeless. Indeed, on 1 November 1897, Chard died, just shy of his fiftieth birthday.

As a recipient of the Victoria Cross, Hook received invites to special occasions and events, and it seems he made every effort to attend them.

On 7 January 1898, Hook received an invitation from Colonel E. S. Browne VC, 24th Regiment, to attend an all-expenses paid commemorative event on 23 January that would see the dedication of a Memorial Brass in the Priory Church (now Brecon Cathedral) which recorded the names of the NCOs and men of the regiment who had lost their lives at iSandlwana.

Every man of the regiment who had fought at Rorke's Drift received an invitation, with the VC recipients being treated as VIPs. Around sixty Rorke's Drift men attended, including Fred Hitch VC, Robert Jones VC, William Jones VC, and John Williams (Fielding) VC.

Taken in January 1898 at Brecon during the memorial brass dedication, this impressive photograph shows the Victoria Cross recipients of the regiment. Henry Hook stands in the centre with Robert Jones standing on the left and William Jones on the right, both of whom had defended another section of the hospital at Rorke's Drift.

Front row L-R: David Bell, whose VC was awarded in 1867 for his actions during the Andaman Islands Expedition; Edward Browne, who was awarded his VC for actions at Hlobane during the Anglo-Zulu War, and John Williams, who had knocked though the walls of the hospital at Rorke's Drift whilst Hook held the Zulus at bay.

Sadly, Robert Jones would go on to take his own life not long after this event. Notable too is the fact that William Jones is not wearing his VC which he had pawned after falling on hard times.

Hook as a Sergeant-Instructor of Musketry in the 1st Volunteer Battalion, Royal Fusiliers.

Together with Frank Bourne and John Williams, Hook would also attend an event in Chard's hometown of Taunton, Somerset, where a memorial was unveiled by Lord Wolseley. Fred Hitch was unable to attend, so family members went on his behalf.

Following the event at Brecon in 1898, a reporter from *The People* visited the British Museum to see Hook. Upon being told that Hook was at home, the reporter found him 'stretched on his bed, with an ice-water bandage round his forehead, and, literally his martial cloak around him.'[99]

Hook informed the reporter that Rorke's Drift had taken it out of him and that he often went down with ague fever. On this occasion the doctor diagnosed 'cephalalgia' (headache). Hook, in fact, had been suffering terrible headaches for a while, and several years prior had suffered from an abscess to the head. During an interview shortly before his death, Hook described being wounded in the head by the assegai, noting that, although it didn't trouble him much at the time, it had caused him 'a great amount of illness since.'[100] Certainly it had left a scar which was prominent throughout his life.

The attendant at the British Museum, who takes charge of the hats and coats. Few people know that he is James Hood, V.C., with whose heroism all England was ringing at the time of Rorke's Drift, in the Zulu War.

Henry Hook in 1904. Note the mistake in the newspaper caption (*Daily Mirror*, 5 July 1904) which erroneously states Hook's name as 'James Hood'.

Hook took part in a carnival for Widows' and Orphans' Fund in St. Pancras in which he played the part of General Buller in the procession.

Hook's health continued to deteriorate and in 1904 his doctor recommended a change of climate, preferably to the countryside, away from London's smoke and smog. Years of dusting books in the library couldn't have helped. His lungs, it seems, were worn out.

GEN. SIR REDVERS BULLER, V.C.

Hook bore distinct similarities to General Redvers Buller who, as a major, had been awarded the Victoria Cross for gallantry in the Zulu War. During (or slightly after) the Boer War, a newspaper reported: 'In appearance Hook bears a strong resemblance to the now famous General. He has the same shaped head, the double chin, the close-set kindly eyes surmounted by the same shaggy eyebrows, and the prominent under lip shaded by the drooping grey moustache that has been made so familiar.
What makes the illusion more complete is the military-looking peaked cap that Hook wears as a Museum attendant.'

Knowing the end of his working life was fast approaching, Hook applied to the paymaster at Brecon for an increase in his VC pension on the grounds of ill-health and underwent a medical examination. Whilst awaiting a decision, Hook, now with little choice available to him, ceased his employment with the British Museum. On 31 December 1904, Henry Hook, after almost twenty-five years with the museum, resigned from his position 'on account of failure of health.'[101]

Shortly after Hook's retirement, he was notified that his application for an increase in his VC pension to £50 a year, paid quarterly in arrears from January 1905, had been approved. After being forced to retire ten years earlier than the standard retirement age without a pension from his employer, this must have come as pleasing news. Since Hook had no pension and was bound to struggle financially, subscriptions from well-wishers began to raise him some much-needed capital.

Hook, on 23 January 1905, then resigned from the Royal Fusiliers, and the following day received a letter from George Barwick, the Superintendent of the Reading Room in the British Library, stating he was 'sorry to hear that your health has been so bad, but trust the fresh air of the country will gradually restore you.'[102]

Barwick's letter was wishful thinking. Hook had doggedly continued to work and to serve in the volunteers until the very end, but tuberculosis had taken hold and Hook would soon be dead.

***

Despite Lord Wolseley's strong and negative views regarding the acts that various Victoria Cross recipients–particularly those at Rorke's Drift–had performed, he must have felt something for Hook as an individual. Over the years he had supported him through references and had requested to see him during his visit to the museum. Now, together with Lord Chelmsford, he contributed to a subscription fund set up to help Hook after his forced resignation.

The fund was created by the *Natal Witness*, which noted that he has no other means to support himself. The paper went on to include a letter of sympathy that was received together with a subscription from a man in Newcastle who had personally met Hook:

> I have read with great interest your article on 'A Stranded Hero' in your issue of the 28th. I have met Sergeant Hook on more than one occasion at the door of the British Museum, where he was employed in a humble capacity, taking charge of umbrellas and walking-sticks which visitors brought with them. I was invariably greeted by our hero with a genial smile and bon homme.
>
> None of the typical hero about him, just an ordinary looking individual. On one occasion I heard it remarked, 'he doesn't look much of a soldier.' However the fact remains that it was Sergeant Hook who saved the wounded in the hospital at Rorke's Drift from all the fiendish overtures of the Zulus.[103]

The article went on to say that praise Hook's gallant service, writing that he 'should be saved from the workhouse, and have his last few years made happy.'[104]

7

THE DEATH OF A HERO

On the advice of his doctor, Hook and his family moved to Gloucester, into rented accommodation at 2 Osborn Villas (connected to Roseberry Avenue), where it was hoped the country air would help his condition. They arrived towards the end of January, but a short time later, on 12 March, Hook passed away, age fifty-four.

The cause of death was given as 'pulmonary consumption 6 months' (tuberculosis).[105] Evidently, Hook had been living on borrowed time, and no amount of fresh air would have saved him from the inevitable.

Hook's death was reported the next day in *The Citizen*, a local paper, and in London papers the day after that. Letters of sympathy soon began to arrive, including one from John Williams (Fielding) VC who, in the letter to Hook's wife, Ada, called Hook his old friend his 'Comrade-in-Arms'.[106] Another letter from a Rorke's Drift defender (thought to be Fred Hitch VC) was also received.

Hook was buried the following Saturday, 18 March, 1905. The funeral was on a grand scale and the streets were lined with thousands of well-wishers as the huge procession made its way to Hook's final resting place. The police led the way, with a firing party, and volunteer band with drummers and buglers behind them. Next came the gun carriage with bearers from the South Wales Borderers (formerly the 24th Regiment of Foot) with pall bearers from the Royal Fusiliers, and numerous detachments of rifles, engineers and artillery. Carriages of chief mourners included Hook's family, representatives of the Odd Fellows, and his loyal friend Fred Hitch VC. Finally, the procession arrived at St. Andrew's Church in Churcham, and Hook was laid to rest.

Hook's funeral where entire streets were filled with mourners.

His grave had been 'lined with laurel, bay and oak, the symbols of victory and of valour in saving life.'[107] An apt symbol of Hook's devotion to his comrades in the stuffy confines of the hospital at Rorke's Drift back in January 1879.

8

REMEMBRANCE

Following the death of Hook, attention soon turned to how to honour his memory and immortalize his name. A brass memorial plate measuring 28" x 21" was placed in Brecon Cathedral on the west wall. Similar plaques reside on this wall, and Hook is the only non-commissioned man among them, the others being his old commanding officer, Major-General Henry J. Degacher; Major-General Sir Wilsone Black (who, as a major, had taken on Hook as his servant at Rorke's Drift); Major-General Sir William Penn Symons who, as a captain, had written up his detailed battle-report at Rorke's Drift and who had died from gunshot wounds in the Second Boer War; and Lieutenant-General Richard T. Glyn who had been the column commander for the central invasion force of Zululand. A plaque dedicated to Hook's former company commander, Major Gonville Bromhead, who had died in 1891, resides in a separate section of the cathedral.

Further, a subscription by the Vicar of Churcham raised funds for a six-foot high white marble cross to be installed at the head of Hook's grave. The ceremony took place eighteen months after Hook's funeral. Additionally, another subscription raised some much-needed funds for Hook's wife and young daughters. The money was of help but was not enough to support his girls who would be sent to the Royal Soldiers' Daughters' Home.

The unveiling of the marble cross placed at Hook's grave some eighteen months after his death.

Hook's gravestone (Wilf Charles)

It was unusual for a man of Hook's rank to be honoured with a plaque alongside the high-ranking officers of the regiment, but this was not the only honour given in such a way. It was also highly unusual for a private soldier to appear in *Who's Who*, yet in 1899, he was approached by the publication to feature in it. Contributions were by invite only, and a person could not request to be included. Entrants had to supply their own entry and Hook's was very modest, with basic information about his military service and not much else. He omitted all mention of his family and of his employment history outside the military. As was normal practice, his entry appeared each year until his death.

Not long after Hook had died, the regiment had approached Ada to express their interest in purchasing Hook's Victoria Cross. At the time, despite her financial troubles, Ada had kept the VC, but, almost twenty years later, in 1924, she made the decision to contact the regiment about the possibility of selling it to them. They offered her £50, which she accepted. Ada sent Hook's South Africa campaign medal as a part of the sale, and both medals are now held by the regimental museum in Brecon.

Hook's second wife, Ada Hook, and their daughters, Victoria Catherine and Letitia Jean (right). Victoria can be seen wearing her father's miniature Victoria Cross.

In 2017, a new housing development in Churcham, Gloucestershire, named 'Henry Hook Close (VC)' opened. Named in Hook's honour— he is buried in the village churchyard—members of his family attended the opening ceremony along with the Vice-Lord Lieutenant of

Gloucestershire, members of the parish council, and the Two Rivers Housing Association responsible for the build. They were the first new homes to be built in the village for over fifty years.

Plaque to Henry Hook, unveiled in January 2019 for the 140th anniversary of the battle, marking one of his now-demolished residences in Gloucestershire, prior to enlisting. Shortly before the unveiling, Paul Barnett poignantly took the plaque to Rorke's Drift to the spot where Hook had earned his VC. (Paul Barnett)

9

HOOK'S DISCREPANCIES

Primary sources are notoriously full of contradictions and inaccuracies. Nevertheless, they are essential when reconstructing what happened during historical events. It is the job of the historian to decipher what is reliable and what is not.

Not surprisingly, the accounts left by those who were at Rorke's Drift are full of errors, and many of the statements from the defenders contradict others.

Since Hook left more accounts than any other defender it should come as no surprise that many contradictions feature in his multiple descriptions of the battle. A lapse of time, bad memory, and the fog of war, all contribute to inaccuracies. Yet with Hook, other reasons also exist.

Hook was illiterate and his accounts were given verbally, leaving room for the interviewer to perhaps embellish or jot down incorrect information by mistake. At least one of Hook's accounts was edited at the point of transcription. A simple word out of place can change the whole meaning of a statement. Yet, as will be seen, even this cannot explain some of the discrepancies in Hook's accounts.

It is interesting to note that Hook's personal descriptions of the battle were heavily influenced by accounts left by other defenders and that, after reading these accounts, he incorporated information gleaned from them into his own versions, sometimes with inaccurate results.

In 1892, *Historical Records 24th Regiment 1689-1892* was published. The book covered the Battle of Rorke's Drift by reproducing two reports, one from John Chard and the other from Reverend George Smith who had kept the men supplied with ammunition throughout the battle. It seems that Hook 'borrowed' information from Smith's account and much of the finer detail which featured in his subsequent accounts undoubtedly came from this source. It is probably no coincidence that after the release of the book, Hook went into detail describing the names of the trees and shrubs that surrounded the mission station exactly how Smith had described them and that he began to mention the dimensions of the buildings and spoke of the materials used for their construction, exactly like Smith had.

Hook's accounts contradict themselves regarding the supposed plan to retire from Rorke's Drift after they had received news that the Zulus were approaching. In his 1898 account Hook stated that before Chard had arrived from the ponts, the sick were loaded onto two wagons and were going to be sent to Helpmekaar pending Chard's arrival, but the decision was then made not to send them after all in fear of them being caught in the open and overrun. However, by the time of his 1905 account, the story had changed somewhat and Hook now stated that the entire garrison was planning on retiring, not just the wounded as he had initially claimed in his earlier account.

He also mixed up the sequence of events, mistakenly claiming that Chard was present before any decision was made. Multiple sources, however, including Chard himself and also Hook in his own earlier version(s), confirm that the decision to strengthen the post for defence was made whilst Chard was still down by the ponts. This small timing error changes the entire dynamic of the situation and has been responsible for authors and historians claiming that Chard had wanted to flee the station when in fact he wasn't present during the discussion.

Influence from other accounts, editorial edits, nor the passage of time, can be responsible for the contents of a letter that Hook sent to his mother shortly after the battle.

In the letter, Hook related that 'Sergeant Maxfield was burnt alive in the hospital; the enemy swarmed around and burnt the place before we could save him, and as he was raving mad with fever, he could not save himself…'[108]

Later, when Hook returned home from South Africa and was asked by the local reporter in his first interview about Maxfield's death, he gave a different yet still inaccurate version of Maxfield's death.

Sergeant Robert Maxfield was a local man, so it was natural for the reporter to want specifics. Maxfield's mother 'kept a small shop' on a road—Cinderhill Street—by Monmouth town centre, right by the Hook family home.[109] Hook described seeing Maxfield in Monmouthshire 'when he was last home', noting that he was 'a very smart young fellow… but when he got out there the climate did not agree with him, and he was attacked by dysentery, and a kind of rheumatic fever, which made him quite mad.'[110]

The reporter noted that Hook's eyes went 'suspiciously watery' when asked how Maxfield died. 'I think only I know', related Hook:

> Poor fellow, in his delirium he tried to get at the enemy, but I tried all I could to keep him back, having one or two narrow shaves of being killed myself in the attempt; however, all I could do was useless, he got among the crowd of savages, and soon fell wounded, being killed soon after,–not burnt to death as some suppose.[111]

Here Hook changed his story from Maxfield being burned alive to stabbed by the Zulus. However, Hook described being present and witnessing Maxfield's death, but this is untrue. He was not present at the time of Maxfield's death, and Maxfield was not killed whilst attacking the Zulus as claimed by Hook. He was stabbed to death whilst lying on in his bed in a fever-ridden stupor.[112]

Robert Jones was the only man present when Maxfield was killed, and he gave his own account of what happened. John Williams who was with Hook in another part of the building at the time agreed with Jones, stating that Robert Jones made a gallant attempt to rescue Maxfield, 'but the sergeant was killed with assegais before he could carry him off.'[113] Many other accounts from those who took part in the battle support the version of Jones and Williams. Indeed, Hook himself later switched his own story to agree with how everyone else who was there described it.

In his interview for the *Royal Magazine* in 1905, for example, Hook, after explaining the fight in his own section of the hospital, noted that 'Privates William Jones and Robert Jones during all this time were doing magnificent work in another ward which faced the hill':

> They kept at it with bullet and bayonet until six out of the seven patients in that ward had been removed. They would've got the seventh–Sergeant Maxfield–out safely, but he was delirious with fever, and, although they managed to dress him, he refused to move. Robert Jones made a last rush to try and get him away like the rest; but when he got back into the room he saw Maxfield was being stabbed by the Zulus as he lay on his bed.[114]

Frustratingly, Hook's reasons for his constant change of story will remain a mystery.

***

In Hook's early account to the local reporter, he gave the following description of finding Maxfield's body after the battle:

> I was able to identify him [Maxfield] after because I knew where he fell and he had a blue check shirt on; there wasn't much left to identify–only a piece of his shirt as large as a lady's handkerchief, and a small part of his body, all the rest was burnt. But (with a fiery flash of the eye), the man who killed him was killed and fell in the fire. But I don't like talking of these things.[115]

Interestingly, in the movie, *Zulu*, released over 80 years after the battle, Maxfield's death scene would be almost identical to how Hook described it in his first inaccurate account. Is it possible the writers had this account to hand? Perhaps not, but if so, it would mean that Hook has given historians and screenwriters the run-around, contributing to an incorrect reconstruction of the hospital fight where it was wrongly believed–owing to Hook saying he was with Maxfield when he was killed–that Hook and Williams had linked up with the Joneses when knocking through the walls.[116]

Although short in length, Hook's first account contains yet another unexplainable discrepancy. 'In the smoke' noted Hook, 'I did manage to carry seven out of the nine who were with me to a place of safety'–the other two were killed.[117]

The implication here is that Hook seems to suggest that he personally carried seven men to safety. Yet we know from his many subsequent accounts and from others that this is not true. He personally carried one man–Private Connolly–to safety.

Hook also gave an interesting yet inaccurate depiction of the hospital evacuation when he said: 'Grasping a pick, I rapidly made a small hole in the dry, sun-burnt brick partition, and dragged several sick and wounded men through into the next ward'–whilst in other accounts he more accurately says he held the door whilst Williams dragged them through.[118]

An interesting and sometimes overlooked aspect of the evacuation is that Hook and Connolly did not know each other; Hook being a

member of 'B' Company 2/24th, and Connolly belonging to 'G'
Company. At least one author has vented his disappointment that
Connolly did not mention Hook by name as his rescuer when
recounting his escape from the hospital. Yet the same can be said for
Hook, who did not name Connolly in his earlier accounts, referring to
him simply as a man with a broken leg or similar.

Connolly and the other wounded and sick were moved to
Helpmekaar directly after the battle, leaving no time for Hook and
Connolly to speak to each other. Hook evidently discovered the name
of Connolly at some point, probably after reading of it elsewhere, as
by the time of his later accounts he was referring to him by name.

***

Hook never went into too much detail about the native patient he left
behind when he retired to the neighbouring room, but his accounts do
show that he could not have been forced out of the corner room
because of fire or smoke as claimed in more than one account.

In 1891 when describing the fate of the native, Hook stated: 'There
was only one patient in my room with a broken leg, and he was burnt,
and I was driven out by the flames, and was unable to save him.'[119] In
his account for the *Royal Magazine* in 1905 Hook described the native
pleading and begging not to leave him behind, with Hook stating: 'Fire
and dense choking smoke forced me to get out and go into the other.
It was impossible to take the native patient with me.'[120]

After moving out of the corner room Hook stood for a while behind
its internal door which he later defended with bullet and bayonet. After
the Zulus had forced an entry into the corner room Hook described
hearing them speaking with the native whom, he said, was asked a
series of questions before being killed. Hook did not attempt to
remove the native from the corner room prior to the Zulus getting in.

However, although Hook claimed that the native was burnt, he later
contradicted this by saying he heard the Zulus speaking to him before
killing him.[121]

He also admitted to later re-entering the room—something that he
couldn't have done if it was ablaze and he had already been forced out
because of the fire which had already burnt the native alive—where he
found and killed a young Zulu who was making off with his things.[122]

However, in an account from 1898 Hook is forced out of the room
owing to the Zulu attacks being too much for one man to deal with,

69

and his gun jamming. Since the room had two loopholes–the other having been initially made for Cole–it would have been impossible for Hook to cover both sides of the room at once.[123] This would make sense and seem far more plausible reason for him moving rooms. Curiously, in that account, there is no mention of the fire being a reason.

The observations above highlight the confusing and often contradictory nature of primary sources and should serve as a reminder that a first-hand account of an event does not necessarily mean an accurate description of the truth. The accounts not only from Hook, but from everyone involved in the battle–and indeed from any historic event in time–most likely contain inaccuracies and inconsistencies. This is by no means a slur on Hook. Far from it, the aim of the exercise is to show the difficulty with sources when trying to reconstruct events. Inconsistencies like this are commonplace. It's just that due to Hook leaving so many accounts, these inconsistencies become more apparent.

10

ZULU

When one considers Hook's portrayal in the movie, *Zulu*, it can be understood why his family were annoyed. The film was released in 1964 and featured an ensemble cast, with the actor James Booth playing the part of Hook.

In the movie, Hook is something of a malingerer--a rogue-come good--who is inaccurately portrayed as a patient in the hospital. His character in the movie has no wish to fight a battle and refuses to take part until persuaded to do so by his comrades already fighting for their lives. He is seen as a heartless thief, a gambler, a criminal, and a man very fond of alcohol. His commanding officer, Lieutenant Gonville Bromhead--played by Michael Caine--scorns at the fact that he has been given a rifle.

To this end, James Booth plays the part perfectly. Described as having 'a punchy blend of toughness, potential evil and irresistible charm,' Booth's performance is exceptional if not accurate.[124] When questioned about the stark difference in character between the real Hook and his character portrayal, Booth explained that 'the decision to play him as the rebellious barrack room lawyer was forced upon the production team by the backers in Hollywood who required a villain.'[125]

In later life, when describing his character, Booth, who at the time had lived in America for many years, said:

> He was a villain, a rebel--a guy who stuck his fingers up at the world, and didn't like discipline, which most people don't like, and liked to drink. He saw the ludicrous side, but when it came down to it, he fought the good fight and helped save the day. It may be something to do with the British character. When you've lived abroad for twenty-five years as I have and come back, you

see what a strange lot the Brits are–they really are odd. I think that's why they like Hook, he was such a cheeky bastard, but when it came to it he fought and saved his mates.'[126]

Actor James Booth playing Hook in the movie, *Zulu*.

His screen portrayal is a two-edged sword in that it has made him a famous household name, yet in a manner not befitting the real man. James Booth admitted:

> I didn't do any research on the real Hook, I just played him the way it was written. Cy [Enfield–the director, co-writer, and co-producer of *Zulu*] wanted a sort of ne'er-do-well, which suited me–it was the sort of character I played. When the picture came out most people liked that character, except the Hook family– they hated it. The company got a letter from the family complaining about the way I'd played him. They actually sent me a photograph of him–even now it's up in my hallway. He looked like a typical working class Victorian gentleman, a big fat guy with a big bushy moustache, and not the layabout that I played.[127]

A myth exists that claims Hook's daughter stormed out of the premiere in disgust at her father's portrayal. Despite numerous online websites and forums claiming this, there is no hard evidence at all to suggest that it happened. In fact, although she was by no means pleased, his daughter, Letitia Jean Bunting (*née* Hook) attended at least two screenings of the movie.

Attending the A B C Cinema, Gloucester, last evening to see the film "Zulu" are (from the left): Mr. J. Bunting, Mr. D. Western (manager), Capt. A. J. Summerell, of A Squadron Royal Gloucestershire Hussars, the Mayoress (Mrs. Cooke), the Mayor (Coun. Ben Cooke), Mrs. J. Bunting, of Littledean—whose father Sgt. Hook, won a V C in the action at Rorkes Drift in the film, and who is portrayed by James Booth—the City High Sheriff (Coun. J. Holohan), and Mrs. Holohan. Sgt. Hook was christened at Churcham Church and is buried there.

Members of Hook's family with dignitaries at the Gloucester screening of *Zulu*. Contrary to popular belief, there is no evidence to suggest Hook's daughter, Letitia Jean Bunting–seen here (third right) looking less than impressed–did not storm out of the cinema. (Sheldon Hall)

A further myth that the family sued, or tried to sue, the film studio is equally false, although they did write a strongly worded letter of complaint.

In August 2005, during the rededication of Hook's grave, Zulu movie expert and author of *Zulu: With Some Guts Behind It*, Sheldon Hall, made the following address which raises some interesting points:

First of all, might I say what an honour it is to be invited here today to take part in this service in memory of a great man and to be asked to speak before you. If you'll forgive me for harping on my professional interests, I think most of us who are not connected to the Hook family were first introduced to the name of Henry Hook through his portrayal in the film Zulu. Those of us who love the film—and there are many—also came to love the colourful, reluctantly heroic rogue played so brilliantly by James Booth.

Of course, as we came to realise the more we read and learned about Rorke's Drift, the real Henry Hook could scarcely have been more different. A teetotaller, the hospital cook and by all accounts a model soldier, he was nothing like his fictional portrayal. But in 1963, relatively few people were even aware of the battle. Certainly James Booth knew nothing of the real Hook: he simply played the character as written in the script, created out of the writer John Prebble's historical imagination. Prebble was well aware that his creation bore little relationship to actuality, though he also said at the time that very little was then known about the defenders of the mission station. Incidentally, Prebble conducted his research in the Reading Room of the British Library, where in later life Hook had worked as a cloakroom attendant.

But James learned the truth about his character when the film company received not only a letter of complaint from the Hook family, which was passed on to him, but a photograph of the real Henry Hook, which James kept and hung on the wall in his hallway. It remains there still, more than forty years later.

When I accepted my invitation to attend today's service, I suggested…that it might be a nice gesture to invite James also. I hoped that it might serve as the opportunity for a reconciliation—if reconciliation were still needed—with the Hook family. Sadly, as I'm sure everyone here knows, James cannot be with us. On the very day that Roger wrote to invite him here, he died suddenly, at the age of 77.

If James' portrayal still rankles with some people here, perhaps they should remember that without it, and without the film, many of us might never have known about Rorke's Drift at all, never discovered a passionate interest in past events, and never learned the name of Private Henry Hook. Perhaps then, while we honour his memory and celebrate his life and heroic achievement, we might also spare a thought for the man who brought him wider fame and who led us, by a roundabout route, to the truth about the battle and to the man many people regard as its greatest hero.[128]

APPENDIX - DIAGRAMS

Diagrams showing the various stages of the hospital evacuation with the movements of Hook and the other men tasked with defending the patients. (Eric Thornton)

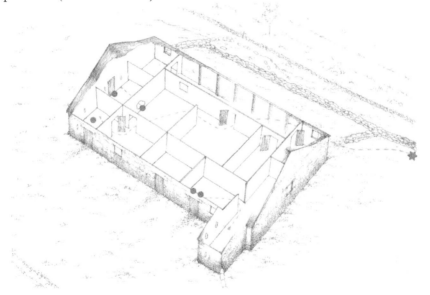

Hook maintains his position in the corner room on the left-hand facing end of the hospital. The route of Private Cole can be seen as he heads from the room with Hook through the hospital and out the front door where he will be shot and killed, although quite where and when cannot be clarified.

Meanwhile, in the room next door, Joseph Williams defends the door. When he is dragged out, John Williams will break through the wall.

Meanwhile, at the other end of the hospital, William Jones has moved through to helps Robert Jones defend the outer doorway from determined Zulu attacks.

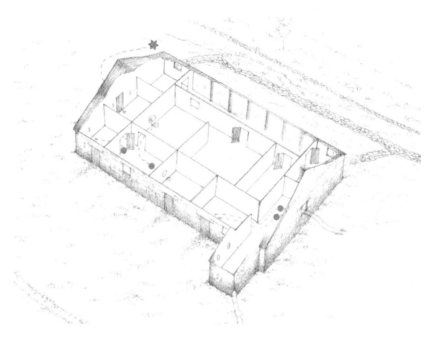

Hook has moved from his corner room into the neighbouring room
which held a group of patients. John Williams has joined him and begins
breaking through the next wall along the rear of the building. Joseph
Williams has been dragged outside and killed.
The Joneses evacuate.

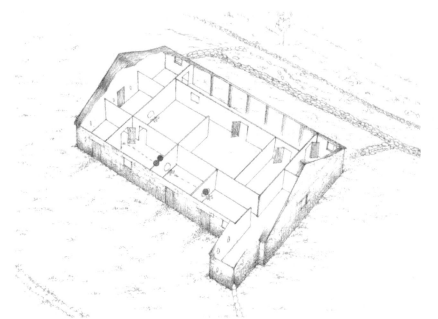

John Williams breaks through to the end room with the patients. Hook
lags behind with Connolly.

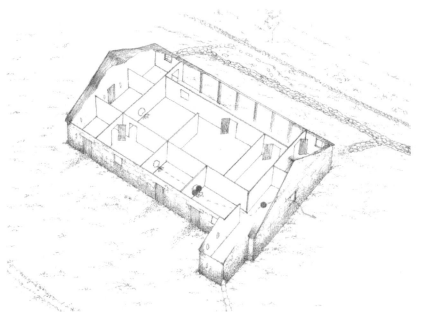

John Williams and the patients escape from the window into the yard
and make their way into the inner defences. Meanwhile, Hook continues his
fighting retreat whilst dragging Connolly with him.

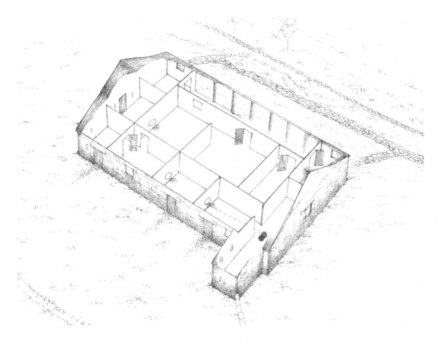

Hook and Connolly enter the final section of the hospital before escaping. The nature of the escape differs depending on the account, making it difficult to know precisely how it happened and which route they took.

ENDNOTES

1. Other notable characters in the movie who differ tremendously from reality are Ass. Comm. James Langley Dalton, Pte. Fred Hitch, C/Sgt. Frank Bourne, and Lts. Chard and Bromhead, as well as Otto Witt (who wasn't actually present during the battle).
2. Bancroft, J., in *Zulu War VCs* provides Helen and Eleanor as alternatives.
3. *The Beacon*, 5 June 1964. The article noted that Hook 'was brought before them for poaching and given the option of going to prison or joining the army.'
4. Streatfield, F. N., *Kafirland: A Ten Months' Campaign* (London: Sampson Low, Marston, Searle & Rivington, 1879).
5. Chard, J. R. M., to the Queen, Jan 1880, The Royal Archives.
6. Hook, H., *Strand Magazine*, Vol. 1., Jan-June 1891.
7. Gardner, Capt. A., Official Statement, 26 Jan 1879, National Archives, W033/34.).
8. Reynolds, Surgeon J. H., *Army Medical Department Annual Report for the Year 1878*, Appendix V. Note: Reynolds failed to mention the presence of Waler Dunne in this account.
9. *Ibid*. Note: Although Reynolds himself did not claim this in his own accounts, a second-hand statement from a Mr. Walter Spencer which featured in his obituary in the *British Medical Journal*, 19 March 1932 claimed: 'When fugitives from Isandhlwana reached Rorke's Drift, it was first proposed to evacuate the place, but Reynolds declared that to be impossible.'
10. *Ibid*.
11. Hook, H., *Macmillan's Magazine*, May to October 1898 (Note: account is not written in the first person).
12. *Ibid*.
13. Smith, Rev. G., *Natal Mercury*, 7 April 1879, letter written by Smith on 3 February 1879.
14. Hook, H., *Macmillan's Magazine*, May to October 1898.
15. *Ibid*. Note: In a further account, after he had raised the alarm in camp, Hook stated that they 'were at once fallen in and set to work to strengthen the post...', making no mention of any planned retirement.

Strand Magazine, Vol. 1, Jan-June 1891.

16. Hook, H., *Royal Magazine*, February 1905.
17. Anstruther, Maj. P. R. extract from a letter quoted in *Rorke's Drift: A New Perspective* by Neil Thornton, National Army Museum.
18. Reynolds, Surgeon. J., op. cit.
19. *Ibid.*
20. Hook H., *Royal Magazine*, February 1905.
21. Chard, J. R. M., op. cit.
22. Private Fred Hitch, in an account published in *Chums–An Illustrated Paper for Boys*, 11 March 1908, Hitch related:

'Just before the barricades had been completed the friendly niggers began to funk it, and as soon as they found out that the Zulus were really coming down upon us in great force they commenced to sneak away. We tried to rally them, but it was no use. Then their captain went after them with the intention of bringing them back; but he disappeared too. Just to show these black gentlemen what we thought of their conduct, some of us, including myself, sent a few shots after them, which brought down dead one of their white non-commissioned officers.'

Reverend Smith in his letter dated 3 February, published in the *Natal Mercury*, 7 April 1879, wrote:

'The garden must have soon been occupied, for one unfortunate Contingent corporal, whose heart must have failed him when he saw the enemy and heard the firing, got overt the parapet and tried to make his escape on foot, but a bullet from the garden struck him, and he fell dead within 150 yards of our front wall.'

Hook may or may not have been in the hospital at this point.

23. Hook, H., *Strand Magazine*, Vol. 1., Jan-June 1891.
24. Hook, H., *Royal Magazine*, February 1905.
25. Jones, W., *Strand Magazine*, Vol. 1., Jan-June 1891.
26. Jones, W., *Manchester Evening Chronicle*, 9 February 1911.
27. Bourne, F., *The Listener* magazine. Transcript of his 1936 BBC radio broadcast from 20 December 1936.
28. Hook, H., *Royal Magazine*, February 1905.
29. Hook, H., *The Sketch*, 20 April 1898.
30. Hook, H., *Royal Magazine*, February 1905.
31. *Ibid.*
32. Morris, D., *The Washing of the Spears* (London, Jonathan Cape, 1966).

33. Hook, H., *Strand Magazine*, Vol. 1., Jan-June 1891.

34. *Ibid.*

35. Hook, H., *Royal Magazine*, February 1905.

36. *Ibid.*

37. *VC*, extract, c. 1904.

38. Hook, H., *Royal Magazine*, February 1905.

39. Hook, H., *County Observer* & *Monmouthshire Central Advertiser*, 21 May 1881.

40. Hook, H., *The Sketch*, 20 April 1898.

41. Thornton, N., *Rorke's Drift: A New Perspective* (Stroud: Fonthill Media, 2016).

42. Hook, H., *Royal Magazine*, February 1905.

43. *Ibid.*

44. Hook, H., *Macmillan's Magazine*, May to October 1898.

45. Connolly, J., Statement from a letter by Captain Liddell, Royal Archives, Windsor, RA VIC/034/64 (by kind permission of His Majesty King Charles III).

46. Reynolds, *Surgeon J. H., Army Medical Department Annual Report for the Year 1878, Appendix V.*

47. *Herald of Wales, Swansea Herald* & *Monmouthshire Recorder*, 26 February 1887. Note: In this account, Connolly refers to the man who saved his as 'Jones' who, according to Connolly, was suffering from 'brain fever.'

48. Hook, H., *Macmillan's Magazine*, May to October 1898.

49. Hook, H., *Strand Magazine*, Vol. 1., Jan-June 1891.

50. *Ibid.*

51. *Ibid.*

52. Hook, H., *The Sketch*, 20 April 1898.

53. Hook, H., *Strand Magazine*, Vol. 1., Jan-June 1891.

54. Hook, H., *Royal Magazine*, February 1905.

55. *Ibid.*

56. Hitch, F., *Chums—An Illustrated Paper for Boys*, 11 March 1908.

57. *Royal Magazine*, February 1905. Note: The VC regiment's VC recipient, Private William Griffith, was killed in action at iSandlwana.

58. Hamilton-Browne, Col. H., (Maori Browne) *A Lost Legionary in South Africa* (London: T. Werner Laurie, 1912).

59. Hook, H., *Royal Magazine*, February 1905.

60. Hook, H., *County Observer* & *Monmouthshire Central Advertiser*, 21 May 1881.

61. Johnson, B. C. *Hook of Rorke's Drift* (Birmingham: Bartlett's Press, 2004).

62. Hook, H., *South Wales Weekly Telegram*, 18 April 1879.

63. Harford, Col. H. C. *The Zulu War Journal* (Barnsley: Pen & Sword Books Ltd, 2014).

64. Bromhead, G., Official Letter recommending men of his company for the Victoria Cross, National Archives, London, W032/7390.

65. Degacher, Lt.-Col. H. J. Official letter that accompanied Bromhead's

recommendations (see end note 64), National Archives, Lond, WO32/7390.

66. Rorke's Drift VCs: Lts J Chard & G. Bromhead, Surg-Maj. J. Reynolds, Ass. Comm. J. L. Dalton, Cpl W. Allen (or Allan), Privates F. Hitch, H. Hook, R. Jones, W. Jones, J. Williams, Cpl. F. Schiess.

67. Hook, H., *County Observer* & *Monmouthshire Central Advertiser*, 21 May 1881.

68. *Times of Natal*, 11 August 1879.

69. Hook, H., *County Observer* & *Monmouthshire Central Advertiser*, 21 May 1881.

70. *Natal Witness*, 4 February 1905.

71. It was in fact Melvill who saved the Colour. Coghill tried to save Melvill, although accounts of the time refer to both of them in the same context of the Colour.

72. Wolseley, G. J., *South African Journal, 1879-1880*, edited by A. Preston (Cape Town, A. A. Balkema, 1973).

73. Hook, H., *Royal Magazine*, February 1905.

74. Hook, H., *County Observer* & *Monmouthshire Central Advertiser*, 21 May 1881.

75. Equivalent of £2670 in today's money. Official Data Foundation: UK Inflation Calculator: GBP from 1751 to 2023 (in2013dollars.com).

76. Certificate in the Furness Collection, as referenced in Johnson, B. C. *Hook of Rorke's Drift* (Birmingham: Bartlett's Press, 2004).

77. *Colonnade*: Staff Magazine of the British Museum, No. 13, 'Henry Hook, V.C,: Rorke's Drift Survivor & B.M. Attendant,' November 1967, quoted in Johnson, B. C. *Hook of Rorke's Drift* (Birmingham: Bartlett's Press, 2004).

78. See Johnson, B. C., *Hook of Rorke's Drift* (Birmingham: Bartlett's Press, 2004) for a detailed breakdown of the inaccuracies surrounding this part of Hook's life.

79. Quote from Hook's granddaughter who provided recollections from her own mother, from Johnson, B. C. Hook of Rorke's Drift (Birmingham: Bartlett's Press, 2004).

80. The 1871 census records show Hook as 'Head of Family' with Comfort's parents, John and Anne Jones, as 'Boarders'.

81. Johnson, B. C., *Hook of Rorke's Drift* (Birmingham: Bartlett's Press, 2004).

82. Information gleaned from interviews and conversations with family members, as referenced in *Ibid*.

83. *Ibid*.

84. *Ibid*, quoting *The Beacon* article.

85. *Ibid*.

86. Staff Applications & Testimonials, 1835-1935, memorandum by C. Pulman, 30 September 1880. British Museum Archives, quoted in Ibid.

87. Original in Furness Collection, reproduced in *Ibid*.

88. Furness Collection, referenced in *Ibid*. Card dated 3 September 1881. Hook was invited for his medical on 27 October and was informed that

if he passed, he would be expected to sail the next day.

89. *Ibid.*

90. *Volunteer Service Gazette*, 7 February 1885, cane in the Furness Collection.

91. Medal in the Furness Collection.

92. Furness Collection.

93. This was two-volume set published called *The Life of John Churchill Duke of Marlborough to the Accession of Queen Anne* (London: Richard Bentley & Son, 1894).

94. *Daily Chronicle*, 30 June 1893.

95. 'How VCs are Won: Private Hook at Rorke's Drift', in *V.C.*, 5 November 1893, Furness Collection.

96. Vizetelly, E., *The Sketch*, A Hero of Rorke's Drift, 20 April 1898.

97. Johnson, B. C., *Hook of Rorke's Drift* (Birmingham: Bartlett's Press, 2004).

98. Furness Collection, letter from Charles E. Chard to Hook, 29 October 1897.

99. *The People*, *c.* Jan 1898.

100. Hook, H., *Royal Magazine*, February 1905.

101. Standing Committee Minutes, British Library, 10 December 1904. Hook's last day was 31 December 1904.

102. Furness Collection, letter from G. F. Barwick to Hook, dated 24 Jan 1905.

103. Johnson, B. C., *Hook of Rorke's Drift* (Birmingham: Bartlett's Press, 2004).

104. *Ibid.*

105. *The Citizen*, publication of death certificate, 13 March 1905.

106. Furness Collection, letter from John Williams to Mrs Hook, 14 March 1905.

107. Johnson, B. C., *Hook of Rorke's Drift* (Birmingham: Bartlett's Press, 2004).

108. *South Wales Weekly Telegram*, 18 April 1879.

109. Johnson, B. C., *Hook of Rorke's Drift* (Birmingham: Bartlett's Press, 2004).

110. A 'West-country' newspaper cutting, dated 21 May 1881. Furness Collection.

111. *Ibid.*

112. See *Rorke's Drift: A New Perspective* (Stroud: Fonthill Media, 2016) by N. Thornton for the new accepted hospital evacuation theory confirming it occurred in two distinct (separate) stages.

113. *Evening Express*, Cardiff, 6 June 1896.

114. Hook, H., *Royal Magazine*, February 1905.

115. A 'West-country' newspaper cutting, dated 21 May 1881. Furness Collection.

116. In Zulu Maxfield is killed when the roof that is engulfed in flames

collapses on him and a Zulu who is about to stab him. According to Sheldon Hall's *Zulu: With Some Guts Behind It*, several different versions of the scene were touted.

The Original draft had Hook 'coming through into the smoke and the room crowded with triumphant warriors…'

'He heads for three who are plunging their spears into MAXFIELD's writhing body. HOOK kills one with a terrific lunge, wrenches the weapon free and knocks another man down with a brutal butt stroke. The third is about to stab him when he falls from a shot fired by 395 WILLIAMS who had also come through the hole. Smoke has almost darkened the room. 395 WILLIAMS grabs HOOK's arm and pulls him into the hole. As they force their way through HOOK is yelling.

    HOOK
    They killed my sergeant. They killed my bloody sergeant!'

The Final script replaced the last line with the less hysterical 'Where's that bloody sergeant?' as Maxfield yells out for help; Hook can be seen shouting it in the film, from behind a wall of flames as the roof collapses, though the words are barely discernible. Other subsequent revisions have Maxfield still alive when Hook goes back to rescue him, exhorting Hook to greater effort in the struggle, before he dies–as in the film–under falling timbers from the burning roof.

117. A 'West-country' newspaper cutting, dated 21 May 188. Furness Collection.
118. *The Sketch*, 20 April 1898. In this account, hook also says he met Williams on the way through the walls in the hospital which does not tally with any other account.
119. Hook, H., *Strand Magazine*, Vol. 1., Jan-June 1891.
120. Hook, H., *Royal Magazine*, February 1905.
121. In this account Hook does not categorically state the native was stabbed to death but alludes to the fact by saying he heard the Zulus speaking with him and that his death was a merciful one–i.e. he was stabbed instead of burnt to death.
122. There is an outside chance that Hook meant another room to the front of the building, but this is extremely unlikely and the same applies with access not being a problem due to fire.
123. Hook, H., *Macmillan's Magazine*, May to October 1898.
124. *The Independent*, 13 August 2005, James Booth obituary.
125. *The Assegai*, Newsletter of the 1879 Group, December 2002.
126. Hall, S., *Zulu: With Some Guts Behind It*. Expanded & revised 50th

Anniversary Edition (Sheffield, Tomahawk Press, 2014).

127. *Ibid.*
128. Copy of speech supplied to author by Sheldon Hall.

BIBLIOGRAPHY

Books

Bancroft, J., *Zulu War VCs* (Yorkshire: Frontline Books, 2018).

Esdaile, A., *The British Museum Library* (London: George Allen & Unwin Ltd, 1946).

Hall, S., *Zulu: With Some Guts Behind It.* Expanded & revised 50th Anniversary Edition (Sheffield, Tomahawk Press, 2014).

Hamilton-Browne, Col. H., (Maori Browne) *A Lost Legionary in South Africa* (London: T. Werner Laurie, 1912).

Harford, Col. H. C., *The Zulu War Journal* (Barnsley: Pen & Sword Books Ltd, 2014).

Holmes, N., *The Noble 24th* (London: Savannah, 1999).

Johnson, B. C., *Hook of Rorke's Drift* (Birmingham: Bartlett's Press, 2004).

Morris, D., *The Washing of the Spears* (London, Jonathan Cape, 1966).

Stevenson, L., Knight, I., Baynham-Jones A., *Rorke's Drift: By Those Who Were There, Volume I* (Barnsley: Greenhill Books, 2022), *Rorke's Drift: By Those Who Were There, Volume II* (Barnsley: Greenhill Books, 2023).

Streatfield, F. N., *Kafirland: A Ten Months' Campaign* (London: Sampson Low, Marston, Searle & Rivington, 1879).

Thornton, N., *Rorke's Drift: A New Perspective* (Stroud: Fonthill Media, 2016).

Whybra, J., *England's Sons* (Essex, Gift Ltd, 20013) 8th Edition.

Wolseley, G. J., *South African Journal, 1879-1880*, edited by A. Preston (Cape Town, A. A. Balkema, 1973).

Newspapers & Magazines

Cardiff Evening Express.
Chums–An Illustrated Paper for Boys.
Colonnade.
County Observer.
Daily Chronicle.
Daily Mirror.
Herald of Wales.
Macmillan's Magazine.
Manchester Evening Chronicle.
Monmouthshire Beacon.
Monmouthshire Central Advertiser.
Monmouthshire Recorder.
Natal Mercury.
Royal Magazine.
The Beacon.
The Citizen.
The Independent.
The Listener.
The People.
The Sketch.
South Wales Weekly Telegram.
Swansea Herald.
V.C. Magazine.
Volunteer Service Gazette.

Documents/Letters/Other

Army Medical Department Annual Report for the Year 1878.
Ancestry.
British Museum Archives
British Newspaper Archives.
National Army Museum.
The Assegai newsletter.
The National Archives.
The Royal Archives.

ABOUT THE AUTHOR

A recognised authority on the Battle of Rorke's Drift, Neil Thornton has published several books and various articles on the battle and the Anglo-Zulu War in general. His book, *Rorke's Drift: A New Perspective* was a best-seller. He also co-authored *Witnesses at iSandlwana*, the largest compilation of first-hand accounts to be compiled on the battle that preceded Rorke's Drift. He also edited *Rorke's Drift Diary* for The Victoria Cross Trust and produced the foreword.

His non-Anglo-Zulu War titles include *Arnhem Umbrella: Major Digby Tatham Warter DSO*, *Todger*–the biography of Private Thomas Jones VC, DCM of the Cheshire Regiment, *For Conspicuous Gallantry*–based on World War One recipients of the Military Cross, and *Led By Lions: MPs & Sons Who Fell in the First World War*.

Neil is the co-founder and director of Barnthorn Publishing Limited through which this book is published. He also runs a successful property company and has been in the chemical industry for over twenty years.

He lives in Runcorn, Cheshire, with his wife and daughter.

Printed in Great Britain
by Amazon

40917485R00056